D1277982

Kids Around the World Celebrate!

The Best Feasts and Festivals from Many Lands

Lynda Jones

Illustrated by Michele Nidenoff

JOSSEY-BASS
A Wiley Imprint
www.josseybass.com

Published by Jossey-Bass
A Wiley Imprint
989 Market Street, San Francisco, CA 94103-1741   www.josseybass.com

Published simultaneously in Canada.

Design and production by Navta Associates, Inc.

Jossey-Bass books and products are available through most bookstores. To contact Jossey-Bass directly call our Customer Care Department within the U.S. at 800-956-7739, outside the U.S. at 317-572-3986, or fax 317-572-4002.

Jossey-Bass also publishes its books in a variety of electronic formats. Some content that appears in print may not be available in electronic books.

Library of Congress Cataloging-in-Publication Data

Jones, Lynda.
    Kids around the world celebrate! : the best feasts and festivals
  from many lands / Lynda Jones.
        p.   cm.
    Summary: Introduces a variety of festivals celebrated around the
  world. Includes recipes and hands-on activities to give a taste of
  what it is like to be part of a feast or ceremony in another country.
    ISBN 0-471-34527-X (alk. paper)
    1. Festivals—Cross-cultural studies—Juvenile literature.
  2. Holidays—Cross-cultural studies—Juvenile literature.
  3. Multicultural education—Activity programs—Juvenile literature.
  [1. Festivals. 2. Holidays.]   I. Title.
  GT3933.J66   2000
  394.26—dc21   99-14639

Manufactured by Courier Companies, Inc. Westford, MA. USA. 9-09 and subsequent printings.
Cover manufactured by Brady Palmer Printing Co. Carmel, NY. 8-09 and subsequent printings.
FIRST EDITION
PB Printing   10 9 8

Contents

INTRODUCTION	1
WELCOMING THE NEW YEAR!	3
Chinese New Year: China	5
Hogmanay: Scotland	13
Año Viejo: Ecuador	21
New Year's Eve: The United States	26
CELEBRATING BEFORE AND AFTER FASTS	33
Carnaval: Brazil	35
Eid ul-Fitr: Saudi Arabia	42
Carnevale: Venice	48
Mardi Gras: New Orleans, Louisiana, United States	54
GIVING THANKS	63
Pongal: India	65
Iriji: Nigeria	70
Crop-Over: Barbados	78
Thanksgiving: The United States	84
RENEWING THE SPIRIT	91
El Día de los Reyes: Mexico	93
Obon: Japan	99
Hanukkah: Israel	106
Kwanzaa: The United States	114
INDEX	121

Introduction

What would it be like to attend a traditional harvest feast in Nigeria, or to be in a rowdy Mardi Gras parade in New Orleans, or ring in the New Year in Ecuador with a life-size scarecrow? All over the world, kids of every culture celebrate many of the same holidays that you do. While some holidays are celebrated in ways similar to your own, each culture has unique traditions and customs. In *Kids Around the World Celebrate!,* you'll take trips to lots of different countries to learn about some wonderful festivals that children celebrate with their family and friends. The book also includes recipes and other hands-on activities that will give you a taste of what it's really like to be part of a feast or ceremony in another country. Learning about these cultural celebrations is not only fun, but it's also an exciting adventure, and a wonderful way to learn more about people of different cultures, whether they live far away or are your neighbors, friends, and classmates.

Welcoming the New Year!

Everybody loves a party. And the biggest and best party is the one that everyone in the world celebrates: the New Year. People may not celebrate the coming year on the same day that you do. Or in the same way. Depending on where in the world you live, horns blare, firecrackers pop, pots and pans are clanked together, or a pail of water might be thrown out a window. But all of these noisemakers have something in common—they are used to ring in wishes for a joyous and happy New Year!

Calendars

Before calendars were invented, people based their holidays on seasonal changes. For example, they would celebrate a good harvest or the coming of spring. But to know when it's a new year, you first need to have a calendar. Several different calendars are used around the world.

The Gregorian calendar, named after Pope Gregory XIII, who introduced it in 1582, is used in most countries around the world. The pope improved on an ancient Roman calendar, the Julian calendar, that Europeans had been using since 45 B.C. The Gregorian calendar is based on the time it takes the earth to revolve around the sun—365 days, 5 hours, 49 minutes, and 12 seconds—so it's called a solar (sun) calendar. (The time over 365 days eventually adds up to another 24 hours—a leap day. Every four years, a leap day is added to February. That longer year is called a leap year.)

The Chinese calendar is based on the cycles of the moon. That's why it's called a lunar (moon) calendar. It is separated into 12-year cycles instead of 12-month cycles. The Muslim and Jewish calendars are other ancient ways of tracking time. These calendars are divided into 12 months. The length of each month alternates between 29 and 30 days. But these calendars are usually only referred to during Muslim or Jewish religious holidays.

Chinese New Year

-CHINA-

The Chinese New Year celebration is like Thanksgiving, Christmas, the Fourth of July, and Halloween all rolled into one. It is the most important of all the Chinese holidays—a time for families to come together, to pay off all debts, and to make up with friends. It's a time to make a new start filled with hope and good fortune for the future. Homes are cleaned spick-and-span to get rid of any bad luck left over from the past year.

Chinese New Year is celebrated in Chinese communities all over the world, beginning on the first day of the first lunar month of the Chinese calendar (which usually falls sometime in January or February on the Gregorian calendar). The New Year season officially ends with the Lantern Festival, on the fifteenth day of the first lunar month. The Chinese celebrate the New Year with festive costumed parades that include the traditional lion dance and dragon dance. They light firecrackers to scare away any evil spirits that might bring them bad luck in the New Year. During the holiday season, families also give one another gifts, honor their ancestors, visit relatives and friends, and feast on "lucky" New Year foods.

Preparing for the New Year

The Chinese begin their celebration on New Year's Eve. Families shop for food and prepare for visits from their relatives. Many of the foods served symbolize wealth and good fortune. The Chinese may prepare scallion pancakes, dumplings, and plenty of pork, fish, chicken, and vegetable dishes. For dessert they will have sticky rice cakes, pudding cakes, and fruits. Kumquats, apples, and oranges symbolize good luck and are given to friends and family. Families "keep the night" together, eating, drinking, and having fun until New Year's morning.

Honoring Ancestors and Ancient Gods

On New Year's Eve, the Chinese prepare a special altar so they can pray to their family ancestors and a variety of gods. These gods are in charge of good luck, wealth, health, and a long life. The family also burns incense and places a food offering on the altar to please the gods. They pray to the gods of heaven and earth and the Kitchen God, who watches over all families. The Kitchen God reports on every family's good and bad deeds to the Emperor Jade, who is believed to rule over heaven. Some families leave the Kitchen God foods he will like so that he will give them a favorable report. Others prepare sticky rice treats so the Kitchen God won't be able to open his mouth! The result: an excellent chance for a good and prosperous New Year.

Chinese families try to please the Kitchen God, who watches over them.

On New Year's Day the Chinese open their doors to welcome the New Year and the gods who have brought them good luck. Families spend the day visiting friends and relatives.

CHIAO-TZU (DUMPLINGS)

Most Chinese families prepare these special meat-filled dumplings for the New Year feast that they will eat together. It's a custom that is more than 2,000 years old. Here's a simple and delicious recipe for you to try. (Makes 30–40 dumplings)

Here's What You Need

Note: Premade wrappers may be purchased in Asian groceries.

Ingredients
- ☐ 2 cups (473 ml) all-purpose flour
- ☐ ¾ cup (177 ml) cold water

Equipment
- ☐ measuring cups
- ☐ mixing bowl
- ☐ plastic wrap

Chiao-tzu wrappers

Here's What You Do

1 Put the flour in a large mixing bowl.

2 Add water slowly as you mix the dough with your fingers until the dough holds together.

3 Work the dough by using your hands to press and mix it together, forming it into a ball.

4 Place the dough on a lightly floured countertop or pastry board.

5 Use your hands to mix the dough until smooth. Cover with plastic wrap and let it sit half an hour.

6 Split the dough in half. Use half of the dough for the dumpling recipe on the next page, then store the other half in the freezer for the next time you want to make more dumplings.

Chiao-tzu Filling

Here's What You Need

Ingredients
- [ ] 1 cup (237 ml) cabbage, chopped
- [ ] 2 scallions, finely chopped
- [ ] 1 teaspoon (5 ml) salt
- [ ] 1 lb (454 g) uncooked ground beef or turkey or pork
- [ ] ¼ teaspoon (1.25 ml) pepper
- [ ] 1 teaspoon (5 ml) sesame oil

Equipment
- [ ] mixing bowl
- [ ] knife
- [ ] measuring spoons
- [ ] rolling pin
- [ ] large pot
- [ ] slotted spoon
- [ ] adult helper

Here's What You Do

1 Ask an adult to help you chop the cabbage and scallions into small pieces.

2 Place the chopped cabbage in a bowl. Add salt and mix it into the cabbage with your hands.

3 Squeeze the excess water from the cabbage and throw the water away.

4 Add the rest of the ingredients to the cabbage.

5 Roll the dumpling dough into a log measuring about 5 inches (13 cm) long and cut it into 16 to 18 pieces.

6 Flatten each piece of the dough into a circle that has a 3-inch (8-cm) diameter. (Sprinkle the dough with a little flour to prevent sticking.)

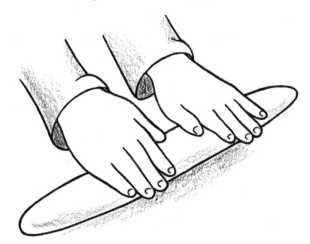

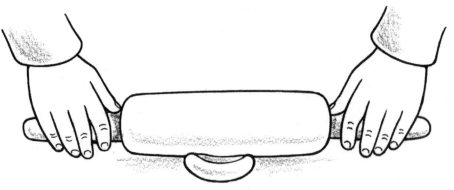

7 Put a teaspoon of the filling in the center of each wrapper.

8 Fold the edges over the filling to form a half-moon shape. Pinch the edges closed with your fingers, making small dents along the edge of the dough.

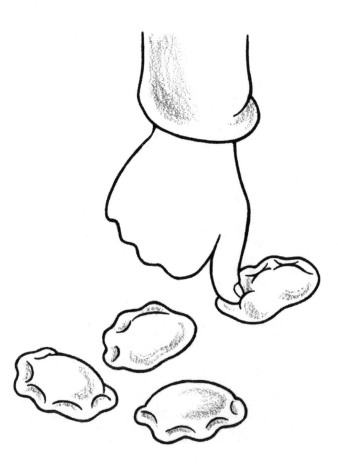

9 In a large pot, have an adult help you bring 3 quarts (3 l) of water to a boil. Add one to two teaspoons of salt to the water.

10 Carefully place the dumplings one by one in the boiling water. Stir to prevent dumplings from sticking.

11 The dumplings are done when they rise to the top of the pot and look puffy. Carefully take them out of the pot, using a slotted spoon, and put them on a serving plate.

12 Dip the dumplings in soy sauce, and enjoy.

Lai-see

Chinese elders and married adults give children and unmarried adults *lai-see,* small square red envelopes filled with money, for the New Year. These envelopes are decorated with beautiful gold Chinese lettering that symbolizes happiness, good luck, health, or wealth.

Spring Couplets

To invite good fortune into their homes, the Chinese hang spring couplets, a pair of long, red paper banners with Chinese characters written on them, on both sides of the entrances to their home. Spring couplets originated more than 1,000 years ago, when Chinese families placed peachwood characters on the gates of their homes. The characters express good wishes for the New Year, and the color red symbolizes happiness. The Chinese also hang around the house squares of red paper on which a single Chinese character is written. The symbol may mean honor, good health, or good fortune. Make your own spring couplets in this activity.

Here's What You Need

- [ ] 6 pieces of red construction paper, 9 by 12 inches (23 by 30 cm)
- [ ] two 14-by-22-inch (36-by-56-cm) pieces of construction paper
- [ ] scissors
- [ ] black tempera paint (available at arts and crafts stores)
- [ ] paintbrush
- [ ] glue
- [ ] string

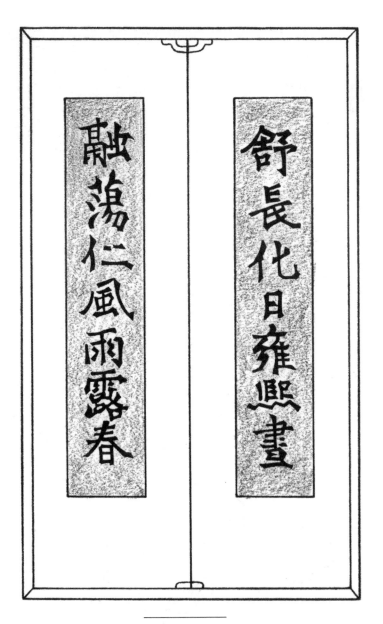

Spring couplets

Here's What You Do

1 Tape three pieces of construction paper together vertically.

2 Paint the Chinese characters onto the banner with the black tempera. (You might try to practice drawing the characters on a piece of paper a few times first.) Let the paint dry.

OR

Enlarge the Chinese characters, shown here, on a copy machine, cut them out, and paste each character onto the construction paper. Let the glue dry. Then go over the symbols with the black paint.

3 Make a stick for the banner by tightly rolling up a 14-by-22-inch (36-by-56-cm) piece of construction paper. To hold the roll together, glue the edge of the end of the paper to the length of the roll. Let the glue dry.

4 Glue the paper stick to the top back of the banner so that it lies about a half inch from the top of the banner.

5 Cut a 28-inch (71-cm) piece of string. Tie one end of the string to one side of the banner's stick. Tie the other end of the string to the opposite end.

6 Repeat steps 1 through 5 for the second banner.

7 Hang the banners from a door or on a wall.

The Chinese express their hopes for a good New Year by displaying these symbols.

Fortune

Honor

Longevity

New Year's Day Parade

In Hong Kong and the rest of China, thousands of Chinese attend a New Year's parade to watch the lion dance and the dragon dance. The Chinese consider the dragon to be the most sacred animal. It is a symbol of strength, long life, and wealth. The lion scares away evil spirits and brings good luck. The dancers underneath the bodies of the lion and dragon costumes control the head and body movements. Unlike Hong Kong and many other cities in China, Taiwan does not have a massive parade. Instead, many small cities have their own parades.

Firecrackers

To make sure the new year will be a good one, it is a Chinese tradition to set off firecrackers to scare away evil spirits. Firecrackers pop at midnight and on New Year's Day. Shopkeepers light firecrackers in front of their stores in hopes that their business will attract plenty of customers and they'll make lots of money in the new year. In some large cities, such as Beijing or Hong Kong, people are not allowed to set off firecrackers because of fear of fires. Instead, families and shopkeepers hang fake firecrackers as a symbol to ward off evil.

Hogmanay

—SCOTLAND—

auld Lang syne ♪ ♪ auld Lang syne

The Scottish are well known for their festive New Year's celebration, *Hogmanay* (pronounced HOG-mah-NAY). This is the most important festival in Scotland—even more important than Christmas. Hogmanay has been celebrated in Scotland since the 1600s. Back then, many religious holidays, including Christmas, were banned because they were believed to be based on superstition.

During the holiday, Scots visit family and friends, bringing gifts of food or whiskey. They celebrate by eating traditional Scottish treats and enjoying a large, festive party to ring in the New Year. The Scots believe that the New Year should begin on a happy note, and that all past problems should be resolved. Hogmanay is celebrated over several days, which gives the Scots plenty of time to recuperate from the festivities.

First-Footing

After the clock strikes midnight, Scots go "first-footing." They visit a friend's or relative's home so they can be the first "foot" to pass over the threshold. Traditionally, the first-footer was a man or boy who was tall, dark, and handsome. This tradition dates back to medieval times, when blond strangers were feared. (Not surprising when you realize that the Vikings, who were blond, fought the Scots for their land.) The first-footer would bring with him a lump of coal, which symbolizes warmth. The visitor would place the lump of coal on the host's fireplace.

In modern times, women are also first-footers, and many visitors do not bring coal. Instead, first-footers may bring food or whiskey, a coin, which symbolizes wealth, or some other token of good luck. In return, the host thanks the visitor with food and drink. The party lasts till the wee hours of the morning.

Why a Hogmanay?

There are quite a few explanations of how the holiday got its name. Some believe the name is from the Celtic New Year called Hogunnus. Others say the name comes from the Anglo-Saxon *Haleg Monath* (Holy Month) or the Gaelic *oge maidne,* which means "new morning."

Feasting

A traditional Hogmanay spread may include cold meats like venison and lamb. Some folks might even prepare a famous Scottish delicacy called *haggis:* sheep lungs, heart, and liver chopped up and mixed with oatmeal and spices, stuffed inside a sheep's stomach (or a plastic bag), sealed, then baked or boiled. It's definitely an acquired taste! This special meal is usually served with "tatties and bashed neeps" (potatoes and mashed turnips). Sweet treats include the all-important sweet loaf that is called black bun (the traditional New Year's cake), Dundee cake (a kind of fruitcake), oatcakes, shortbread, and scones. The Scots also drink plenty of whiskey.

Scones

To get into the spirit of Hogmanay, here's a traditional treat to prepare for your friends. (Makes 6–8 scones.)

Here's What You Need

Ingredients

- [ ] 1 cup (237 ml) self-rising flour
- [ ] 4 tablespoons (60 g) cold butter or margarine, cut up into small pieces
- [ ] ⅓ cup (89 ml) buttermilk
- [ ] 1 egg
- [ ] extra flour for dusting pastry board or counter

Equipment

- [ ] mixing bowl
- [ ] butter knife
- [ ] pastry board (optional)
- [ ] a cookie cutter or small drinking glass
- [ ] rolling pin
- [ ] cookie sheet or shallow pan
- [ ] oven mitts
- [ ] adult helper

Here's What You Do

1 Preheat the oven to 400°F (204°C).

2 Put the flour and butter in the mixing bowl.

3 Mix the butter into the flour with your fingers until it looks like coarse meal.

4 Make a well in the center of the flour mixture; add the egg and most of the buttermilk.

5 Mix thoroughly. (Dough should be soft but not mushy; add more buttermilk or flour if needed.)

6 Use your hands to mix the dough together in the bowl, pressing and working it together with your fingers.

7 Dust a countertop or pastry board with flour and place the dough on the counter.

8 Roll out the dough until it's ½ to ¾ inches (1–2 cm) thick.

9 Cut out circles of dough with your cookie cutter or the rim of a round drinking glass.

10 Ball up leftover dough, roll it out again, and continue cutting circles of dough until none is left over.

11 Lightly grease a cookie sheet or shallow pan with butter or margarine and place the scones on it.

12 Bake in the oven for 10 to 12 minutes, or until the scones are golden brown and firm.

13 Ask your adult helper to remove the scones from the oven. Let them cool.

14 Cut the scones in half. Spread with butter and your favorite jam or jelly. Enjoy them with a cup of hot tea.

Scots play ancient games like "throwing the hammer" during Hogmanay.

Hogmanay Street Fair

Edinburgh (pronounced ED-in-burrow), the capital of Scotland, is host to one of the biggest New Year's Eve parties in the world, including an impressive street fair and carnival that last four days and nights. About 250,000 people attend each year to watch entertainers from all over Europe, eat lots of food, and play traditional Highland games like "throwing the hammer." One of the highlights of Hogmanay is the New Year's Eve Fire Procession, a parade in which everyone carries a torchlight from old Edinburgh to new Edinburgh.

Fireworks and Gunfire

When the clock strikes midnight on New Year's Eve in the center of town in Edinburgh, Scots dressed in their ceremonial *kilts* (pleated plaid skirts) play the bagpipes while others merrily sing "Auld Lang Syne." In other regions of Scotland, fireworks crack, guns blast, and bonfires blaze to ring in the New Year.

Scottish Clans and Crests

In the early days of Scotland's history, many people in the Scottish Highlands, the mountainous northern region of the country, were split up into *clans,* or families. To become a member of a clan you had to share a common ancestor with the clan chief and the rest of the "family." These common ancestors were often legendary heroes, warlords, or kings. Each clan was led by a chief. Clan members adopted the name of their chief, then added the prefix *Mac* or *Mc,* both of which mean "son of." So Scots often have names like MacRobertson or McDonald. Not all Scots' names begin with *Mac/Mc,* though, because many Scots living outside of the Highlands did not belong to a clan.

Scots still take great pride in knowing the meaning of their ancestral surnames (last names) and their clan's *tartan* (plaid pattern) and *crest* (an emblem worn on a helmet or shield that identified what clan you belonged to). The crest designs were fashioned to fit the clan's beliefs or principles. There were no rules for crest designs; the images could be of anything real or imagined and in any color. Some designs included animals, such as a lion, panther, or boar, which were signs of strength; other crests bore signs of swords or arrows, which expressed the clan's readiness to fight. Mythical animals were also popular crest designs: the unicorn is a symbol of purity and virtue, while the phoenix means resurrection and rebirth.

At the top of every crest design is the clan's *motto,* a phrase that expressed their "battle cry" or a guiding

Cameron crest

A Song of Old . . .

On New Year's Eve, people all over the world will sing a song called "Auld Lang Syne." The words for the song were written by a famous Scottish poet named Robert Burns. *Auld lang syne* is Old Scots for "old long ago," or the good old days.

principle. The motto was written in Latin, Gaelic, Norman-French, or English. For example, the Clan Cameron's motto *Aonaibh ri chéile* is Gaelic for "unite"; Clan Sutherland's motto, *Sans Peur,* is French for "without fear."

Sutherland crest

YOUR FAMILY CREST

The earliest surnames were linked to the type of job a person held: Baker, Carpenter, Taylor. The Scottish name Armstrong means "strong arm," and is traced back to a thirteenth-century soldier who saved the king of Scotland in a battle. What's the meaning of *your* surname? Take a trip to the library and look up your surname in a "name book," which lists the meanings of thousands of names from different cultures. Or think about the type of work you'd like to do one day, or a job that a member in your family has that you think is important or fun. Design a crest and construct a shield for your family, using a drawing of a place or thing that symbolizes your name, or something that has great meaning to your family.

Here's What You Need

- [ ] one 12-by-12-inch (30-by-30-cm) piece of colored construction paper
- [ ] markers, crayons, or paint
- [ ] 2 pieces of corrugated cardboard measuring about 22 by 17 inches (56 by 43 cm)
- [ ] tape measure or yardstick (meterstick)
- [ ] marker
- [ ] scissors
- [ ] glue
- [ ] tape
- [ ] 2 large sheets of construction paper, 12 by 18 inches (30 by 46 cm), in a color different from the other construction paper
- [ ] adult helper

Here's What You Do

1 Draw your design on the small piece of construction paper with colored markers, crayons, or paint.

2 Use a yardstick (meterstick) to find the midpoints of three different sides of one of the pieces of cardboard, and mark them *a, b,* and *c.*

3 Draw a line from point *a* to point *b* and a line from point *b* to point *c.*

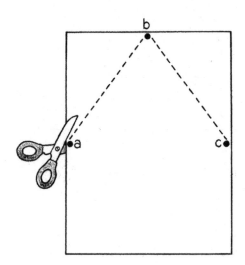

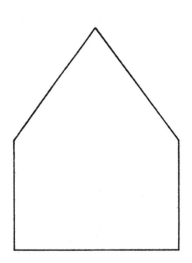

4 Use the scissors to cut through the cardboard along the lines. You may need an adult to help with this.

5 Take the second piece of cardboard, and using a marker, trace the pattern of your first shield onto the cardboard. Cut out the second shield.

6 Measure and draw a 6-by-1-inch (15-by-2.5-cm) slit in the middle of one shield. Cut out the strip of cardboard.

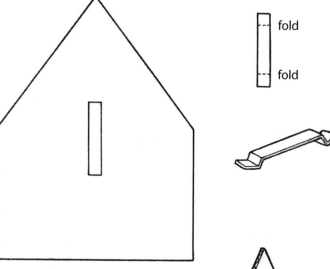

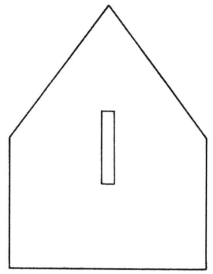

fold

fold

7 Bend the ends of the strip and push each end through the slit of the shield to make a handle. Glue each end of the strip to the back of the shield. Let the glue dry.

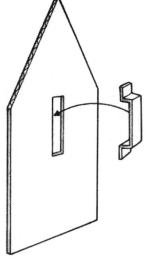

8 Glue the two shields together. Tape around the edges. Let the glue dry.

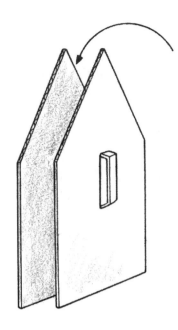

10 Glue your crest design onto the side of the shield covered with construction paper.

9 Glue the large sheets of construction paper onto your shield on the side opposite the handle. Cut off any extra paper around the edges. This will be the background for your crest.

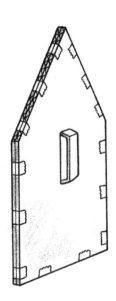

Año Viejo

—ECUADOR—

In South America, the people of Ecuador celebrate the end of *Año Viejo* (pronounced AHN-yo VYAY-ho), the Old Year. This is the time when Ecuadorians can make any bad luck from the old year disappear. Only when the bad luck has "gone up in smoke" can Ecuadorians begin the New Year with a clean slate. Like many of us, they may even make "New Year's resolutions." They promise themselves that they will do a particular thing or complete a certain project.

Noche Vieja (New Year's Eve)

On *Noche Vieja*, New Year's Eve, it is a custom for families to create a life-size puppet or scarecrow that symbolizes the old year. They make the puppet by stuffing rags, paper, hay, and firecrackers into a pair of old pants and a shirt. Next, they make a humorous mask to cover a paper-and-hay head. A tie, hat, pipe, or any other prop that will give the puppet more personality is added. Once the puppet is finished, it is placed outdoors. Then the family writes a "will," a list of everyone's faults, on a piece of paper. At midnight, the church bells ring 12 times to mark the arrival of the New Year. At this time the "wills" are read, then stuffed inside the puppet. A match is lit, and the puppet is set on fire. The firecrackers explode, and the puppet and the "will" with the family's "bad deeds" go up in flames.

Fiesta!!

In Guayaquil, (pronounced Gwy-ah-KEEL), Ecuador's largest city, there is a huge Año Viejo *fiesta* (festival). On New Year's Eve, children carry their child-size puppets through the center of town. The puppets are put on display for everyone to see, and there is a contest to see whose is the best. At midnight, hundreds of puppets are set on fire.

AÑO VIEJO PUPPET

To celebrate Año Viejo, try making your own puppet by using old clothes and newspapers, and writing your "will." While you won't be stuffing your puppet with firecrackers and setting it on fire, you can keep the life-size figure as a festive prop for Halloween or any other holiday.

Here's What You Need

- a month's worth of newspapers
- old pair of pants
- old long-sleeve shirt
- safety pins
- a belt
- a small or medium-size brown paper bag

- markers (any color)
- hat
- scarf
- a chair
- paper
- pencil

Here's What You Do

1 Take a sheet of newspaper, ball it up, and place it aside. Continue balling up newspaper until you have enough to begin stuffing your puppet.

2 Stuff the newspaper into the legs of the pants. Stuff all the way to the bottom of the pant leg and work up. Pack the paper tightly inside the pants.

3 When the pants are tightly stuffed up to the waist, stand the pants up on the floor, letting them lean against a wall.

4 Stuff the tails of the long-sleeve shirt into the waist of the pants. Use safety pins around the front, sides, and back to secure the shirt to the pants.

5 Stuff newspapers into the shirt and the sleeves until they reach the shirt neck.

6 Put the belt around the puppet's pants.

7 Take a small- or medium-size brown paper bag and fill it three quarters of the way with newspaper. Twist it closed and stuff the twisted end into the middle of the newspaper in the shirt neck.

8 Use the markers to draw a pair of eyes, a nose, a mouth, and ears on the bag.

9 Accessorize your puppet with a big hat or a scarf.

10 Seat the puppet in a chair.

11 On a piece of paper, make a list of all the things you regret doing in the past year. This is your "will."

12 When the clock strikes midnight on New Year's Eve, read your will, then throw it away. Now your New Year will get off to a fresh start.

The Año Viejo Feast

Ecuadorian families gather together to prepare and then enjoy the New Year's Eve feast, which is served at 1 A.M. While foods vary from region to region, a New Year's Eve dinner might include turkey or ham, a hen, *humitas* (ground corn steamed in corn leaves), seafood, a *colada* (a thick soup made with meat or chicken), or *locro* (a stew made from milk, cheese, and potatoes), or *llapingachos*, potato and cheese fritters. Before midnight, kids might eat small *empañadas* (meat-filled pies) or thick-sliced fried *plátanos* (a type of banana).

Fried foods are a favorite of Ecuadorians, but they also enjoy an abundance of available fresh vegetables and fruits because of the tropical climate.

ENSALADA DE FRUTAS (FRUIT SALAD)

For dessert on Año Viejo, kids may eat an *ensalada de frutas* (fruit salad) made from banana, mango, pineapple, passion fruit (*maracuya*), honeydew melons, or cantaloupes, and strawberries. Enjoy making this light and sweet dish for dessert, or an energizing quick snack. (Makes 2–4 servings.)

Here's What You Need

Ingredients
- [ ] 1 package fresh strawberries
- [ ] 1 large mango or 2 small ones
- [ ] 1 banana
- [ ] 1 honeydew melon or cantaloupe
- [ ] 1 small can of diced pineapple

Equipment
- [ ] large bowl with lid
- [ ] dinner knife
- [ ] paring knife
- [ ] adult helper

Here's What You Do

1 Rinse the strawberries and then use your dinner knife to slice them in half. Place them in the bowl.

2 Ask your adult helper to peel, pit, and cut up the mango into bite-size pieces. Add to the bowl.

3 Peel the banana and then, with your dinner knife, cut the banana into slices. Add to the bowl.

4 Open the can of pineapple chunks and drain off the liquid. Add them to the bowl. Mix thoroughly.

5 Put the lid on top of the bowl and place it in the refrigerator for two hours, or until chilled.

6 Enjoy your *ensalada de frutas.*

ensalada de frutas

New Year's Eve

Americans nationwide ring in the New Year with a variety of festive activities. Many celebrate by attending private parties or large festive gatherings in public spaces, and feasting on food and drink until the wee hours of New Year's Day. Though Americans celebrate the holiday in similar ways, those living in the North, South, East, or West also have their own special ways to celebrate New Year's Eve.

New York City is host to the biggest New Year's Eve bash in the world. More than half a million people show up and three million more worldwide watch the festivities on TV. New Yorkers and visitors from all ethnic backgrounds huddle together in Times Square—the Crossroads of the World—to watch a huge, lighted ball from atop One Times Square being lowered at exactly midnight to the street. As the giant glittery ball slowly slides down a 77-foot flagpole, everyone counts down the final seconds to the New Year. *Five, four, three, two, one . . . Happy New Year!* Confetti falls, balloons sail, and the loud sounds of noisemakers and excited voices pierce the air. Friends, family, and total strangers hug, kiss, and wish each other a Happy New Year.

For those at private parties or just celebrating at home, it's traditional to ring in the New Year with a glass of champagne. Many also sing "Auld Lang Syne" (see p. 17 on Hogmanay) and make New Year's resolutions, goals they set for themselves for the coming year.

First Night

In Boston, about two million adults and kids attend First Night, the city's annual celebration of the beginning of the new year. The event, which lasts from early afternoon to midnight, is a big indoor and outdoor fair that takes place all over the city. Every year about 1,000 artists and 250 performers get into the act. It's a night when kids can get their faces painted, wear masks and costumes, see puppet shows, dances, laser shows, musical performances, plays, and much, much more. It's also a night to stuff yourself with salty pretzels, hot dogs and sausages, and pizza and hot chocolate. In the evening, thousands of marchers participate in a magical parade, and at midnight, Bostonians are treated to a fantastic fireworks show that takes place over Boston Harbor.

First Night, which began in 1976, was the idea of Boston native Clara Wainwright, who was looking for a fun and exciting alternative for families and others who didn't want to go to a rowdy New Year's Eve party. Wainwright's idea was such a hit that other American cities, and even other countries, have adopted the First Night celebration.

Big Party Planning

The annual New Year's Eve party in New York takes a lot of planning. A "ball drop committee" takes care of every little detail. A ball designer decides what type of lighted designs will be featured on the ball. Then it's fitted with thousands of rhinestones, flashing strobe lights, and powerful lamps that create beautiful light patterns. Colored lights are also connected to the top floors and roof of One Times Square, and about 30 searchlights are set up to rotate around the Times Square area, creating a wonderfully exciting and festive atmosphere.

To increase the party madness, two tons of confetti are released by confetti "cannons," which are set up on 13 different Times Square buildings.

To get New Yorkers into a party mood, the city provides free party favors. They dole out 30,000 colorful five-foot balloons, silver pom-poms and leis, and confetti bags to the crowd. Revelers can scoop up the falling confetti to take home as a holiday souvenir. When the party ends and the partygoers leave Times Square, there's a major mess left behind. Throughout the night, a sanitation team cleans up the debris.

History of the Times Square Ball Drop

The first big Times Square bash was in 1904, when the owners of One Times Square threw a rooftop party to welcome in the New Year. In 1907, New Yorkers saw their first "ball drop" celebration. The publisher of the *New York Times* newspaper came up with the idea not only to celebrate the New Year but also to mark the completion of the *Times'* new neighborhood headquarters. Since then, the spectacle has become bigger and more exciting as the city has added computerized equipment.

Thousands of people gather at Times Square to watch the New Year ball drop.

New Year's Eve Noisemaker

To ring in the New Year in New York style, make this papier-mâché New Year noisemaker.

Here's What You Need

- several newspapers
- ½ cup (118 ml) flour
- 1 teaspoon (5 ml) salt
- ½ cup (118 ml) water
- measuring cup and spoon
- large bowl or small bucket
- a balloon
- cardboard tube (from a roll of toilet paper)
- scissors
- masking tape
- dried beans, any variety
- ½ cup (118 ml) flour
- 1 teaspoon (5 ml) salt
- ½ cup (118 ml) water
- white latex paint
- gouache (opaque water-color paint) or poster paint or glitter pens
- paintbrushes
- clear varnish (optional)

Here's What You Do

1 Tear the newspaper into strips and put them in a neat pile.

2 To make the papier-mâché paste, put ½ cup (118 ml) flour and 1 teaspoon (5 ml) salt into a large bowl or small bucket. Slowly stir in the ½ cup (118 ml) water.

3 Stir the mixture until it's thick and smooth.

4 Blow up a balloon to the size of a large orange. Tie the balloon.

5 Dip a newspaper strip into the paste. Remove the excess paste from the strip with your fingers.

6 Smooth the first strip onto the balloon. Continue pasting the strips onto the balloon, leaving a space the size of a nickel at the bottom of the balloon.

7 Paste on four more layers of strips. (For each layer, alternate the direction in which you lay down your strips. First lay the strips down vertically, then horizontally. This will help you see where one layer ends and the other begins.)

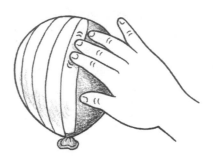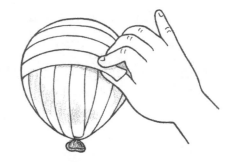

8 Let the papier-mâché ball dry for two to three days. Put it in a safe place to prevent the balloon from popping.

9 When the papier-mâché ball is dry, pop the balloon with a pin and shake it out.

10 Take a handful of beans and pour them through the hole in the ball.

11 Cover the hole with tape.

12 Make a batch of papier-mâché paste, and cover the taped hole with four layers of papier-mâché strips. Let dry.

13 Cut one side of the cardboard tube open.

14 Make the tube smaller by rolling it up.

15 Tape the edges of the tube together with masking tape. This will be the handle for your noisemaker.

16 Attach your cardboard handle to the papier-mâché ball with masking tape.

17 Cover the opening at the handle's bottom with masking tape.

18 Make another batch of paste, following steps 2 and 3.

19 Cover the handle and the area between the noisemaker and handle with three layers of newspaper strips and paste. Let dry.

20 Cover a work space with newspaper. Paint the noisemaker with white latex paint. Let the paint dry.

21 Paint or draw a design on your noisemaker. You might paint on swirls, or write Happy New Year in different colors or with a glitter pen.

22 Finish your noisemaker by glazing it with a coat of clear varnish (optional).

New Year's Day Bowls and Parades

On New Year's Day many American families are glued to their TV sets. Football fans love New Year's Day because it's jam-packed with college football games. These games are called championship bowls. For instance, there's California's Rose Bowl and the Southwestern Cotton Bowl. You can also cheer for the players in the Fiesta Bowl, the Orange Bowl, the Sugar Bowl, and many others.

New Year's Day is also a day for festive parades. The Mummers' Parade takes place in Philadelphia, Pennsylvania, where thousands of people in colorful costumes march on Broad Street in a carnival-like parade that includes fancy floats and groups of string bands. (A *mummer* is a person who puts on a mask and performs during festivals. *Mummer* comes from the French word *momer,* to go masked. In ancient Europe, masked performers acted out plays during the holiday season doing *pantomines,* using their bodily gestures and dancing to express a story.) A panel of judges awards cash prizes for the best costumed group and the best string band.

In Pasadena, California, you'll see the most unique and beautiful sight of all—the Tournament of Roses Parade. Corporations, cities, states, and counties sponsor floats made up of petals from roses, mums, marigolds, carnations, or other flowers, as well as plants, seeds, leaves, and wood. Every surface of the float must be covered with natural materials.

New Year Feasting

Some people invite family and friends over for a New Year's brunch. Others serve a festive New Year's dinner. There's really no universal traditional New Year's dinner. Some people make ham, lamb, or roast chicken. Southerners make collard greens and Hoppin' John (rice with cowpeas or, in some cases, black-eyed peas) to bring good luck in the New Year.

HOPPIN' JOHN (COWPEAS AND RICE)

If you want good luck to follow you into the New Year, try your hand at this recipe. (Makes 4–6 servings.)

Here's What You Need

Ingredients
- [ ] 1 cup (237 ml) dried cowpeas
- [ ] 10 cups (2.37 l) water
- [ ] 1/2 pound (227 g) uncooked bacon, cut into bite-size pieces
- [ ] 1 teaspoon (5 ml) salt
- [ ] 1 teaspoon (5 ml) pepper
- [ ] 1 cup (237 ml) rice

Equipment
- [ ] measuring cup
- [ ] large bowl
- [ ] colander
- [ ] large pot
- [ ] measuring spoon
- [ ] wooden spoon

Here's What You Do

1 Pour the cowpeas into a large bowl. Rinse them and discard any damaged peas.

2 Pour in 5 cups (1183 ml) of water and soak the peas overnight in the refrigerator.

3 The next day, drain the peas in a colander and place them in a large pot.

4 Add to the pot 4 cups (946 ml) of water, the bacon, salt, and pepper.

5 Put a lid on the pot. Have your adult helper heat the water to boiling.

6 When the water boils, reduce to a low heat and simmer for about an hour, or until the peas are almost tender.

7 Add the rice and 1 more cup (237 ml) of water to the pot.

8 Put the lid back on and simmer for another 30 minutes, stirring occasionally to prevent the rice and peas from sticking to the bottom of the pot.

9 The Hoppin' John is done when the cowpeas and rice are soft and most of the liquid has evaporated.

10 Serve the Hoppin' John as a side dish with your dinner, or with a green leafy vegetable, such as collard greens or spinach.

Celebrating Before and After Fasts

*F**asting,* which is giving up food for a certain amount of time, is an important part of many religions. People fast to remind themselves how it feels to go without something that they take for granted. Fasting is also a way to make up for bad deeds done in the past. For Lent, the 40 days of fasting that lead up to Easter, Christians promise to give up certain foods, such as meat and sweets. That's why they celebrate the days before Lent by drinking, eating, dancing, and having lots of fun. These celebrations are known as carnival throughout the world. *Carne vale* is Latin for "farewell to meat." In New Orleans, the last day before Lent is called *Mardi Gras,* which means "Fat Tuesday." The first day of Lent is called Ash Wednesday.

Muslims in Arab countries and around the world observe a fasting period that is called *Ramadan*. Muslims fast for 30 days, at the end of which they celebrate *Eid ul-Fitr* (pronounced EED ool-FEET-er), the Festival of the Breaking of the Fast, by eating lots of rich foods while they enjoy the company of friends and family.

Carnaval

Carnaval in Rio occurs over the three days before Ash Wednesday, which begins Lent. During carnaval Brazilians forget about work and concentrate on the *samba,* the percussion (drum) music and two-step dance of Brazil.

35

This national dance was created by the country's Afro-Brazilians, whose three to four million African ancestors were brought by the Portuguese to Brazil and enslaved between 1538 and 1850. The Afro-Brazilians are responsible for the samba and many other traditions that make carnaval a unique, fun, and festive celebration. Today Brazilians of all colors celebrate the festival by wearing elaborate costumes and partici-

pating in local parades and feasts all over the country. The most well-known and most popular parade takes place in Rio.

There are about 16 samba schools that participate in the main carnaval parade (the number of schools varies from year to year). They are the best performers in Rio. To prepare for the big event, the *Cariocas* (pronounced car-ee-OH-kahs) (residents of Rio) write music and songs, make costumes and floats, and choose themes, usually social, political, or religious, for the parade. The festival lasts from the Saturday to the Tuesday before Lent. Schools shut down for the entire week and kids dress up for the festivities.

Everyone looks forward to the main Samba School Parade, but there are many other parades to see. One is Rio's street

Street Parades

Lesser-known samba schools and locals snake down a designated parade route in Rio's street carnaval. Other schools, such as the Banda de Ipanema (Ipanema Band), have local parades in their own neighborhoods. Sometimes as many as 5,000 people join in. There's no fee to participate. Tourists are invited to put on costumes and join the locals, singing and dancing on the sidewalks and in the streets. In Salvador, another city, rolling flatbed trucks filled with musicians and singers, *trio electricos,* follow behind the costumed marchers.

trio electrico

Musicians and singers ride *trio electricos*— flatbed trucks— and entertain the crowds.

carnaval, where anyone can join a parading club, dress up in a costume, and samba. Thousands of people attend and enjoy local costumed parades that are held in neighborhoods all over Rio, Salvador, Recife, and other parts of Brazil.

Sambódromo

A fierce contest between the best samba schools takes place over two days in the *Sambódromo* (Sambadrome), a giant stadium built in Rio in 1983 for the carnaval competition. Only the best schools are invited to participate. The arena seats up to 85,000 people, but tickets to the event are expensive. Those who can't get tickets stand outside the Sambódromo, watching as paraders enter the stadium, or they can watch the national event on TV. For about 80 minutes, each school shows off its samba steps, music, lyrics, and exotic costumes. A panel of judges rates each school. No one gets to sleep until the last school parades past the judges— sometimes after 5 A.M. the following day. The contestants for the top eight schools are treated like celebrities, appearing on TV and in magazines and newspapers.

Samba Schools

The first samba club was called Deixa Falar, which means "let them speak" in Portuguese. The name of their club was a response to being barred from participating in the main carnaval parade. The club was founded in 1929 and held its first parade the following year. They practiced in school yards because they needed lots of space. That's why samba clubs became known as samba "schools." After the introduction of Deixa Falar, more Afro-Brazilian samba schools formed. Today, while samba schools are made up of mostly Afro-Brazilians, Brazilians of every color can and do participate. Each samba school has from 3,000 to 5,000 participants. A school will easily spend up to one million dollars on floats and costumes. To earn money, schools hold fund-raisers and dances, and sell T-shirts, cups, flags, and other souvenirs marked with the samba school logo and name. Local sponsors also donate money to the school of their choice for the big event.

Mango of the Future

Kids get involved in carnaval, too. Many parents take their kids to the samba schools that they belong to. Most samba schools have a children's "wing," a section of the band in which the children can march. One of the oldest samba schools, Mangueira, has a school just for kids called *Mangueira do Amanha*, which is Portuguese for "mango of the future."

SAMBA SCHOOL FLAG

Every samba school has a *porta-bandeira,* or flag bearer. Traditionally, the flag bearer is a woman and she wears a dress with an elaborate hoop skirt. Imagine that you are the *carnavalesco,* carnaval master, of a new samba school and you need to design a school flag. Think of a name for your school and a symbol or design that would best fit your school's image. The symbol might be an animal, cartoon character, superhero, or a fruit or flower.

The *porta-bandeira,* or flag bearer, carries the Mangueira samba school flag.

Here's What You Need

- [ ] 22-by-14-inch (56-by-36-cm) piece of fabric (polyester, nylon, canvas, cotton) in any color
- [ ] iron
- [ ] marker
- [ ] fabric glue
- [ ] 40-inch- (101-cm-) long stick or wooden dowel, $\frac{1}{4}$-inch (.6 cm) in diameter (available from a lumber or crafts store)
- [ ] cardboard
- [ ] stencils, templates, or shapes cut out from magazines
- [ ] felt (any color)
- [ ] scissors
- [ ] poster paint, markers, or glitter pens
- [ ] press-on stars, glitter, or other decorations
- [ ] adult helper

Here's What You Do

1 Make a ½-inch (1-cm) fold at the top of the fabric. (To keep the fabric folded over, ask an adult to iron it down.) Glue the fold down and let the glue dry. Repeat this step with the bottom and one side of the fabric.

2 With a marker, draw an outline of your design on a piece of cardboard, then cut it out. If you're using cutout images from a magazine, trace around the shapes of the images on a piece of cardboard, then cut them out.

3 Place your cutout design, stencils, or templates on a piece of felt. Trace them and then cut them out.

4 Glue your felt design onto the fabric. Let the glue dry.

5 Take your dowel or stick and roll around it about ½ inch (1 cm) of the edge of the fabric that was not folded down. Fold it around the dowel until it's tight. Glue the edges of the fabric together. Place a heavy book on top of the fabric to keep the fabric stuck together as the glue dries.

6 Use paint, markers, or glitter pens to write your samba school name on the flag.

7 You can further decorate your flag with press-on stars, glitter, or anything else you can think of.

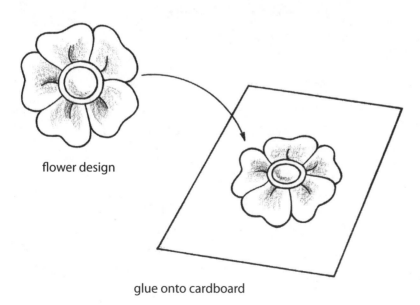

flower design

glue onto cardboard

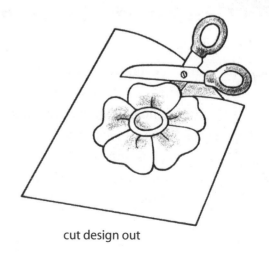

cut design out

Food to Samba By

Street vendors sell many snacks and drinks during carnaval. The types of foods show influences from all of the cultures that make up Brazil—the native Indian peoples, the Portuguese, and Africans. You'll find *acaraje* (fried bean fritters), *bolinhos de queijo* (deep-fried cheese balls), fried codfish balls, steamed corn, popcorn, hamburgers, and hot dogs. Popular drinks are *caldo de cana* (fresh-squeezed sugarcane juice), *guarana* (a popular soft drink made from a Brazilian berry), tropical fruit juices and shakes, and *caipirinha,* a drink made with sugarcane brandy, lime, and sugar.

REFRESCO DE CÔCO (COCONUT COOLER)

Brazilians enjoy the many fruits and vegetables available in their country. At carnaval, you'll find delicious shakes and juices made from cashew, tamarind, guava, passion fruit, or coconut—a favorite of many Brazilians.

Here's What You Need

Ingredients
- [ ] 1 cup (237 ml) canned coconut milk
- [ ] 1½ cup (355 ml) water
- [ ] ¼ cup (59 ml) sugar (or more to taste)
- [ ] 2 cups (471 ml) crushed ice

Equipment
- [ ] large pitcher
- [ ] drinking glasses
- [ ] straws

Here's What You Do

1 In the pitcher, mix the coconut milk, sugar, and water.

2 Add the crushed ice to the pitcher. Stir.

3 Pour the shake into two glasses and serve with straws.

Eid ul-Fitr

—SAUDI ARABIA—

Eid ul-Fitr is a joyous celebration for the people of Saudi Arabia and throughout the Muslim world. It occurs after Ramadan, a 30-day fast during which they strengthen their faith and compassion for the sick and poor. During Eid ul-Fitr, which means "the festival of the breaking of the fast" in Arabic, Muslims thank Allah (God) for giving them the strength to complete the fast successfully. It is a time for forgiving others and beginning again. It is also a time for having fun. For three days, schools and businesses shut down, and Muslims celebrate by eating, dancing, and singing, and visiting friends and relatives.

Eid Traditions

Muslims follow a traditional ritual on the morning of Eid. They put on their new or best clothes, jewelry, and perfume. The household donates food, money, or grains to a charity or a poor family. After they make their offerings, they pray. In the Muslim world, women and men cannot pray together. Usually women pray at home and the men pray at a mosque, a Muslim house of worship. If women do pray at a mosque, they must pray at a mosque for women only, or pray in a separate area from the men. After prayers, Muslims hug one another and say *"eid mubarak,"* which is Arabic for "holiday blessings."

At home, Muslim women prepare delicious feasts for family and friends. During the next two days, families visit each other, starting with the oldest relatives and ending with the youngest.

For children, Eid is especially sweet. They receive gifts of money and new clothes. They look forward to the candy, pastries, and cookies that their families will serve over the three-day holiday.

Eid Feast

Every family makes its favorite foods for the holiday. Lamb and chicken are the most common meats eaten in the Arab world. Eating pork and drinking alcoholic beverages are forbidden by the Koran. For Eid, a typical meal might include a

Who Are the Muslims?

Muslims are followers of the religion of Islam. *Islam* is Arabic for "submission to the will of God," and *Muslim* means "one who submits." Muslims believe in one God, Allah, and in the prophet Muhammad. A *prophet* is a special person who delivers messages from God to others. Islam began with Muhammad, who was born in Mecca (which is now in Saudi Arabia) in A.D. 570. When Muhammad turned 40, he received a vision from the angel Gabriel. He was told to teach his people that there was only one God and that they should worship only God. Muhammad's followers wrote down his words, which were collected into a holy book called the Koran.

Mecca is now considered a very holy place. Five times a day, Muslims all over the world face toward Mecca and the Kaaba, a holy building, to pray. Today, over a billion Muslims worldwide belong to the Islamic religion. It is the second largest religion in the world.

whole roasted lamb stuffed with seasoned rice, dates, apricots, and nuts. Plenty of vegetables, such as a salad, eggplant, olives, and chickpeas, would be served, too. A bowl of yogurt is usually included, as well as Arab bread, called pita. Arabian coffee or tea, *laban,* a yogurt drink, camel's milk, and cola are typical drinks. For dessert, they would serve apples, dates, oranges, and cookies stuffed with dates and nuts.

DATE-NUT COOKIES

These cookies, called *ma'amoul,* are a traditional treat during the Eid holiday. Arab children look forward to making and eating these cookies, and so will you and your family. (Makes 12 cookies.)

Here's What You Do

1 In a medium-size bowl, combine the chopped dates with ¼ pound (.11 kg) of the softened butter. Mix together with a fork or spoon until well blended.

2 Stir the chopped walnuts into the date mixture. Set the bowl aside.

3 Combine the semolina and sugar in a large bowl and mix until well blended.

4 Melt the remaining pound of butter in a small saucepan.

Here's What You Need

Ingredients

- 2 pounds (.9 kg) fresh pitted dates, finely chopped
- 1¼ pounds (.8 kg) butter, softened
- 1 cup (237 ml) chopped walnuts
- 1½ pounds (.7 g) semolina flour (available at health food stores or Middle Eastern groceries)
- 1 cup (237 ml) sugar
- hot water
- powdered sugar

Equipment

- measuring cup
- measuring spoons
- bowls
- fork or spoon
- airtight container
- blender or food processor
- saucepan
- baking sheet

5 Add the butter to the semolina mixture a little at a time. Using your hands, make the dough by mixing the butter and semolina mixture together.

6 Set the dough aside in an airtight container for an hour.

7 After the hour is up, preheat the oven to 450°F (230°C).

8 Add a little hot water, one tablespoon at a time, to the dough to soften it up. Mix the dough with your hands.

9 Form a small ball of dough, then with your hand flatten the ball into a circle measuring about 2 inches (5 cm) in diameter.

10 Make an indent into the center of the dough ball with your finger and fill it with some of the date-nut mixture.

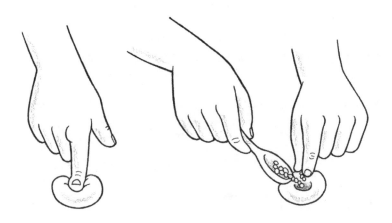

11 Seal the top of the cookie by pulling up the edges of the dough and pressing them together.

12 Flatten the dough slightly to form a cookie shape. Be careful not to let the date mixture ooze out of the cookie.

13 Take a fork and press the tines lightly against the dough to form a design on top of the cookie.

14 Continue making the rest of the cookies.

15 Place the cookies on an ungreased baking sheet and bake for 20 minutes or until golden brown.

16 When the cookies are done sprinkle them with powdered sugar and eat.

Muslim Calendar

Eid can begin at different times of the year and in different seasons. Unlike the Western Gregorian calendar, which is based on the cycles of the sun, the Islamic year is based on the cycles of the moon. Eid begins with the sighting of the thin crescent moon in the tenth lunar month of the Muslim calendar. Religious officials in Saudi Arabia announce the sighting of the new moon to the Muslim community. The information is shared with mosques around the world so that Muslims worldwide can celebrate the festival at the same time.

EID MUBARAK GREETING CARD

During Eid, Muslims exchange colorful greeting cards that are similar to Christmas cards. The cards say *"Eid Mubarak"* ("Holiday Blessings") on the outside. Inside may be the greeting "In this Eid ul-Fitr may there be safety and happiness for all mankind and a peaceful earth." Muslims send Eid cards to their family, friends, and neighbors.

Here's What You Need

- 8½-by-11-inch (22-by-28-cm) piece of poster board (any color)
- two pieces of 8½-by-11-inch (22-by-28-cm) construction paper (any color)
- scissors
- copy of the mosque pattern—see next page
- 8½-by-11 (22-by-28-cm) piece of cardboard
- pencil
- 12 inches of ribbon (any color)
- hole punch
- felt-tip pens
- glue or glue stick
- wrapping paper or old magazines with images of flowers, leaves, stars, moons, or any images you like

Here's What You Do

1 Make a card by folding the 8½-by-11-inch (22-by-28-cm) poster board in half.

2 Cut a piece of construction paper to measure 7 by 5 inches (18 by 13 cm). Put a little glue around the edges and paste the paper to the inside right-hand side of the card. Let it dry.

3 Make a photocopy of the mosque shown here, and glue it onto the piece of cardboard. Let the glue dry. Carefully cut around the outline of the mosque with a pair of scissors to make a pattern.

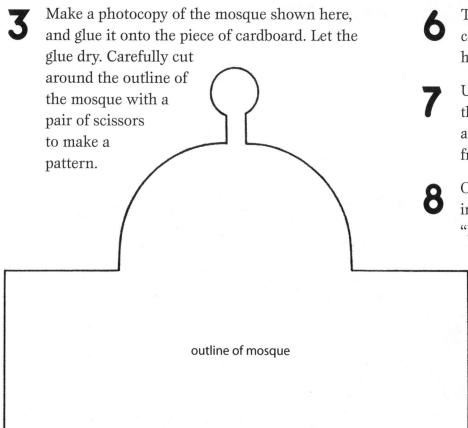

outline of mosque

4 Place the mosque pattern on the second piece of construction paper. Carefully trace around it with a pencil and cut it out.

5 Hold the construction paper mosque at the top of the front of the card, and with your hole punch, make a hole through the card and the mosque.

6 Thread the piece of colored ribbon through both holes and tie a bow.

7 Using a felt-tip marker, write the greeting *"Eid Mubarak"* anywhere you'd like on the front of the card.

8 On the construction paper inside the card, neatly write: "In this Eid ul-Fitr may there be safety and happiness for all mankind and a peaceful earth," and sign your name.

9 To decorate your card, carefully cut out the images from the wrapping paper you chose and glue them to the card.

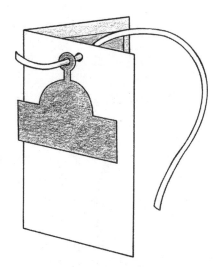

thread ribbon through
punched hole in mosque and card

Carnevale

Venetians, the people who live in Venice, Italy, have the longest celebration of carnevale in the world. For 10 days, they attend dances and masked balls in palaces. They play ancient games and go to grand operas, and they watch or participate in colorful parades. On the final day of carnevale, Venetians board gondolas in the evening and ride up and down the Grand Canal, whose borders are lighted with hundreds of tiny candles. In the final hours of carnevale, fireworks light up the Grand Canal and hundreds of gondolas float along in a colorful procession.

Venetian Gondolas and Canals

Venice is one of the most unusual cities in the world. It lies on 120 islands in the Adriatic Sea. Instead of streets, Venice is crisscrossed by about 150 narrow canals, or waterways. Because Venetians are surrounded by watery "streets," they don't travel around the city in cars or buses. Instead, they hop into *gondolas,* long, narrow boats that are manned by a *gondolier,* a person who pushes the boat through the water with a *sweep,* a narrow oar. Venetians also have speedier ways to get across the canals. Many Venetians take a motorboat taxi or a *vaporetto,* a motorboat that acts as a "water bus." The Grand Canal, the main canal in Venice, links the smaller canals together. For those who like to take a stroll around Venice, more than 400 bridges cross the canals and connect the Venetian islands.

History of Carnevale

Carnevale, which started in Italy in the 1400s, became extremely popular during the sixteenth century. Celebrations began the day after Christmas and continued until the beginning of Lent. Venetians gathered in the Piazza San Marco (St. Mark's Square), a huge open square in Venice. There were boat races on the Grand Canal where people wore elaborate costumes. It was a tradition for everyone to wear masks so that rich and poor people, who otherwise never would have socialized, got to celebrate together. The masks made everyone equal. When Napoleon Bonaparte conquered Venice in 1797, he banned carnevale. Though the holiday was celebrated in the nineteenth century, it didn't regain its popularity until the next century.

Costumes and Masks

Many carnevale masks and costumes that people wear today are based on the medieval outfits worn in the eighteenth century. Now, as then, the most popular costume is the *bautto,* a black silk hood, a silk or velvet cape, a three-horned hat, and a gold, black, or white mask.

In the early days of carnevale, rich and poor Venetians wore the same costumes.

Mask Making

Mask making is a serious craft. There are shops in Venice devoted to making and selling masks, many of which end up as decorations on walls instead of being worn. The most common masks are made from papier-mâché, and some are cracked to give them an antique look, but masks can be made of many materials, such as porcelain and even leather. Though vendors can sell masks year-round, masks are only worn during carnevale.

PAPIER-MÂCHÉ MASK

Many carnevale masks represent characters from the *commedia dell'arte*, which means "comedy of art," Italian comedies that featured masked performers. The troupe of characters in these plays were symbols of good or evil. Some well-known characters were Arlecchino (Harlequin), a childlike, lovesick acrobat; Coviello, a musician; Pantalone, a miserly merchant; and Punchinello, a fat hunchbacked clown with a large hooked nose. Each character's mask and colorful costume fits its personality. Other characters you'll see are long-nosed

Pinocchios and court jesters, people who earned their living by making jokes, asking riddles, and telling funny stories to royal families.

In this activity you'll be making your own medieval Venetian mask. What better way to get into the spirit of carnevale?

Venetian craftsmen design and make a variety of beautiful masks.

Here's What You Need

- several newspapers
- ½ cup (118.2 ml) flour
- 1 teaspoon (5 ml) salt
- ½ cup (118.2 ml) water
- measuring cup and spoon
- large bowl or small bucket
- balloon
- pin
- scissors
- Magic Marker
- sharp knife
- white latex paint
- poster paint
- paintbrush
- clear varnish
- elastic thread
- adult helper

Here's What You Do

1 Spread some newspapers over your work surface. Then tear the rest of the newspapers into strips. Save the strips in a neat pile.

2 To make the papier-mâché paste, put the flour and salt into the large bowl or small bucket. Slowly stir in the water. Keep stirring the mixture until it's thick and smooth.

3 Blow up the balloon until it's about the size of your head. Tie the end off.

4 Dip a newspaper strip into the paste. Remove the excess paste from the strip with your fingers, and smooth the strip onto the balloon mold from top to bottom.

5 Continue pasting the strips onto the balloon, lengthwise, until you have covered only half of the balloon.

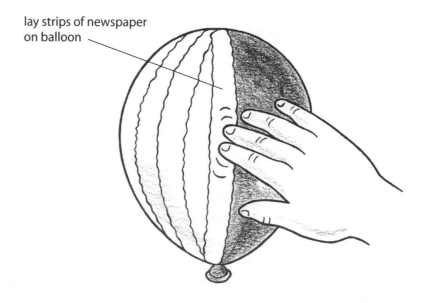

lay strips of newspaper on balloon

6 Paste on four more layers of strips. (For each layer, alternate the direction in which you lay down your strips. First lay the strips down vertically, then horizontally. This will help you see where one layer ends and the other begins.)

7 Let the mask dry for two to three days. Put the mask and balloon in a safe place to prevent it from popping.

8 When the mask is dry, pop the balloon with a pin and remove the balloon.

9 Trim the edges of the mask with scissors to even it out.

10 Draw eyes on your mask with a Magic Marker and ask an adult to cut them out with a sharp knife.

11 Paint the inside and outside of the mask with one layer of white latex paint. Let the paint dry.

12 Paint the outside of the mask with poster paints in any designs you like. Let the paint dry.

13 Paint the mask with two coats of clear varnish. Let the varnish dry between each coat.

14 Ask an adult to use a knife to make a small hole on each side of the mask. Pull the elastic thread through the holes and adjust it to fit the size of your head.

Carnevale Food

During carnevale, Venetians make a special treat, called *fritelle,* sweet fritters made with raisins and pine nuts or lemon peel. They also have plenty of pizzerias or cafeterias that serve fast Italian food and a variety of *panini,* sandwiches. *Tramezzini* are triangular sandwiches made with decrusted white bread, slathered with mayo or some other sandwich topping, and filled with *prosciutto,* Italian ham, cheeses, salami, *mortadella* (a lightly smoked sausage), grilled chicken breast, tuna, mozzarella, and tomatoes, or anything else you want. There are also delicious Italian pastries, and *gelato,* Italian ice cream.

TRAMEZZINI

These sandwiches are great for lunch or a quick snack between meals. Spread out some Italian lunch meats and cheeses and make a variety of *tramezzini*. Invite some friends over to share them with you. (Makes 6 small sandwiches.)

Here's What You Need

Ingredients

- [ ] Italian lunch meats and cheeses, such as salami, mortadella, prosciutto, provolone, mozzarella
- [ ] tomato, lettuce, and onion
- [ ] your favorite sandwich spread
- [ ] 6 slices of white bread

Equipment

- [ ] sandwich knife
- [ ] cutting board
- [ ] plate

Here's What You Do

1 Lay out your sandwich fillings and spreads on a table or countertop.

2 Use your sandwich knife to cut each slice of bread into a square shape. Throw away the crusts and excess bread.

3 Slather some sandwich spread onto one slice of bread. Pile some sandwich fillings on top of it, then put the other slice of bread on top.

4 Cut the sandwich into two triangles.

5 Repeat steps 2 through 4 with the other bread slices.

6 Place the *tramezzini* on a plate and eat up.

Mardi Gras

If you enjoy Halloween, you'll love Mardi Gras. During Mardi Gras, the streets of New Orleans, Louisiana, are taken over by a host of costumed characters—princesses, medieval knights, clowns, soldiers, animals, flowers, and cartoon characters. *Mardi Gras* (pronounced MAR-dee-grah), which is French for "Fat Tuesday," is the last day of the carnival season in New Orleans, which begins on January 6. It is the final day to party before Ash Wednesday, the beginning of Lent.

Big, rowdy parades and masked balls lead up to Mardi Gras, but the biggest parade takes place on Mardi Gras day. It's an official holiday, and the whole town shuts down. Every year more than a million people gather along the parade route on St. Charles Avenue to watch masked riders on decorated floats and local marching bands pass by. The parade lasts from 11 A.M. to midnight. The locals call Mardi Gras the "greatest free show on earth."

Carnival Krewes

The first New Orleans *krewe,* a masking and parading club, was called the Mystic Krewe of Comus. *Comus* comes from the Greek word *komos,* which means "revelers." The group was formed by a group of white men in 1856. Over the next few years, more krewes were formed. In 1872, a group of white businessman founded the Krewe of Rex and planned a Mardi Gras parade in honor of the visiting Grand Duke Alexis Romanoff of Russia. Rex adopted the Romanoffs' royal colors as the official carnival colors: green (faith), gold (power), and purple (justice).

Though Rex, Mystic, and other krewes held yearly parades and balls, they were not open to everyone. Italians, Jews, and blacks were not invited to join many of the parades or attend the balls. Many krewes still discriminate today. In 1909, a group of African American men formed the first black parading club, the Zulu Social and Pleasure Club.

It wasn't until after World War II that Mardi Gras really took off and many other groups of people—doctors, servicemen, lawyers,

Mardi Gras in the New World

The French celebrated Mardi Gras in Europe long before New Orleans was founded. Then on March 3, 1699, French-Canadian explorer Sieur d'Iberville and his men camped 60 miles (9.6 km) from what would become New Orleans. March 3 just happened to be Mardi Gras day that year, so d'Iberville named the campground Point du Mardi Gras. When more French came to the New World and settled what is now Louisiana, they kept the Mardi Gras custom alive, even after Louisiana was purchased by the United States in 1803. They feasted and held masquerade balls before Lent. By the early 1800s Mardi Gras had become so rowdy that both the celebration and wearing masks were outlawed. But New Orleanians ignored the laws and celebrated anyway. By 1826, Louisiana officials caved in, and both Mardi Gras and mask wearing were legalized.

businessmen, and neighborhood groups—formed their own krewes and joined the parade. Today, there are about 130 krewes in New Orleans, but only 60 krewes actually take part in parades during carnival; the rest hold parties and balls. Each krewe can include as few as 50 people or as many as 800. Every year a king, queen, and captain are chosen to preside over the masquerade balls and parades. The captain is in charge of organizing the events. Today there is a parading club for everyone, including one for dogs, called Barkus. The dogs wear costumes and ride in decorated wagons pulled by their owners.

The Black Indians

In the late eighteenth century, the Louisiana Chickasaw Indian tribe helped hide a group of escaped black slaves, saving them from certain death. African Americans in Louisiana passed down this story from generation to generation. In the 1880s, African Americans and descendants of Native Americans formed their first carnival club, which they called the Creole Wild West Tribe. Today there are over 20 African American and Native American parade clubs, or *tribes*. The Mardi Gras Indians are the most anticipated sight of carnival. Their elaborate Indian costumes are made up of tremendous feathers, rhinestones, and sequins.

The Black Indians wear the most colorful and elaborate costumes at carnival.

"Throw Me Sumtin', Mista!"

Paradegoers don't come just to watch the parade, they come to participate. As decorated floats pass by, the masked riders toss a variety of Mardi Gras trinkets, called *throws,* to the parade watchers. Throws are plastic bead necklaces, doubloons (fake coins inscribed with the krewe's name), cups, or the hard-to-get hand-painted coconuts, which are tossed into the crowd by the Zulu Krewe. Eager parade watchers try to get the attention of the masked riders by waving and yelling, *"Throw me sumtin', mista!"* Special Mardi Gras ladders with a bench on top can be bought from local hardware stores. Parents set up these ladders to help kids not only enjoy the parade but also catch the "throws" more easily.

CARNIVAL BEADS

Strands of colorful bead necklaces are the one thing you'll see everyone wearing at carnival. Some are silver. Some are gold. Others are multicolored. The necklaces are a symbol of Mardi Gras revelry. Bead throwing evolved from the tradition of the krewes throwing any old object from a float to their "subjects" during carnival. In 1988, the Coconut Bill was passed in New Orleans to include the fruit as a tossable item. This bill spared krewes from being held responsible if the hard nut hit someone. Like all the unique throws tossed during carnival, the beads go hand in hand with Mardi Gras, and they're fun and easy to make.

Here's What You Need

- beading thread (any color)*
- small colored plastic beads*
- size no. 10 beading needle*
- glue
- scissors

*available at a bead shop or art supply store

Here's What You Do

1 Cut 3 26-inch- (66-cm-) long pieces of beading thread. Put two strands of thread aside.

2 Make a knot at one end of the remaining piece of thread.

3 String the beads one at a time onto your thread. Use a beading needle to string the beads if the thread is not stiff enough.

4 Continue beading until 2 inches of thread are left.

5 Hold one end of the thread in each hand. Draw the 2 pieces together and tie a double knot. Snip off any excess thread.

6 Repeat steps 1 through 5 to make two more necklaces. When the beads have all been used, place your throws around your neck and enjoy the spirit of Mardi Gras.

Mardi Gras Foods

It is a custom for Louisianians to eat king cake, a traditional dessert made during the carnival season, from January 6 to Mardi Gras Day. The cake is named after the three magi who traveled from the East to see baby Jesus. King cake is a wreath-shaped coffee cake decorated with colored sugar in the carnival colors: purple, green, and gold. Inside the cake is a tiny plastic pink baby doll. Louisianians host king cake parties throughout the carnival season. Whoever gets the slice with the doll inside has to throw next year's king cake party.

While king cake is the only food Louisianians serve especially for Mardi Gras, you'll still enjoy the variety of Louisiana cuisine. It is unique because of the unusual cultures that influenced it, including the *Creoles* (pronounced CREE-oles), Louisianians born to French or Spanish parents; and the *Cajuns* (pronounced CAY-juns), French Acadians who settled in Louisiana. Native Americans and West African slaves also contributed to the delicious cuisine. The Indians introduced the French to corn, dried beans, and cereals, while the West African slaves introduced them to *guingombo,* or okra. *Guingombo* is an ingredient used in the traditional Mardi Gras gumbo, a peppery stew. In addition to okra, gumbo includes seafood or chicken and usually either *tasso* (spicy, dried Cajun ham) or *andouille* (Cajun sausage). Red beans and rice is another popular dish. Other foods eaten during Mardi Gras are po' boys, which are heros stuffed with fried oysters, shrimp, catfish, or crayfish; *muffuletta*, a 10-inch round sandwich stuffed with lunch meats, cheeses, and topped with a minced olive salad; and boiled crayfish. For dessert there's pecan pie and warm bread pudding topped with a warm rum sauce.

KING CAKE

Get into the spirit of Mardi Gras by making a king cake and hosting a king cake party for your friends. (Serves 10–15)

Here's What You Need

Ingredients

- [ ] ½ cup (118 ml) warm water (110°–115°F) (43°–46°C)
- [ ] 2 packages active dry yeast
- [ ] ½ cup (118 ml) plus 1 teaspoon (5 ml) sugar
- [ ] 4½ cups (1066 ml) all-purpose flour
- [ ] 1 teaspoon (5 ml) nutmeg
- [ ] 2 teaspoons (10 ml) salt
- [ ] 1 teaspoon (5 ml) lemon zest
- [ ] ½ cup (118 ml) warm milk
- [ ] 5 egg yolks
- [ ] 8 teaspoons (120 ml) (1 stick) softened butter, cut into slices

- [ ] 2 tablespoons (30 ml) softened butter
- [ ] 1 teaspoon (5 ml) of cinnamon
- [ ] 1 egg slightly beaten with 1 tablespoon (15 ml) milk
- [ ] 1 1-inch plastic baby doll (available at a craft store or cooking supply store)

COLORED SUGARS

- [ ] green, purple, yellow pastry paste (available at cooking supply store)
- [ ] 12 tablespoons (180 ml) sugar

ICING

- [ ] 3 cups (711 ml) powdered sugar
- [ ] ¼ cup (59 ml) lemon juice
- [ ] 3–6 tablespoons (45–90 ml) water

Equipment

- [ ] small, shallow bowl
- [ ] measuring cups and spoons
- [ ] mixing spoons
- [ ] 2 large mixing bowls
- [ ] kitchen towel
- [ ] pastry brush
- [ ] baking sheet
- [ ] oven mitt
- [ ] adult helper
- [ ] 3 pieces of wax paper
- [ ] medium bowl
- [ ] spatula

Here's What You Do

1 Pour the warm water into a small shallow bowl. Add the yeast and 2 teaspoons (10 ml) sugar.

2 Allow the yeast and sugar to rest for three minutes, then stir the mixture thoroughly.

3 Let the yeast mixture rest for 10 minutes, or until the yeast begins to bubble up and the mixture doubles in volume.

4 In a large mixing bowl, add 3½ (829 ml) cups flour, the remaining sugar, nutmeg, and salt. Combine the ingredients together thoroughly with a spoon.

5 Add the lemon zest and stir.

6 With a spoon, make a well in the center of the flour mixture and pour in the yeast mixture, warm milk, and egg yolks.

7 Slowly combine the dry ingredients with the wet ingredients, mixing thoroughly until the batter is smooth.

8 One tablespoon (ml) at a time, add 8 tablespoons (120 ml) (1 stick) of cut-up butter into the batter. Mix the batter thoroughly after adding each tablespoon of butter.

9 After all the butter is added, continue to mix the batter for about two minutes more, or until the dough can be formed into a soft, medium-size ball.

10 Lightly flour a countertop or pastry board. Turn the sticky dough out onto the counter and mix the dough together with your hands and fingers.

11 Add 1 cup (237 ml) more of flour to the dough, a tablespoon (ml) at a time. Sprinkle a tablespoon (15 ml) of flour over the dough, then mix it into the dough with your hands and fingers.

12 Continue adding the flour and mixing the dough until the flour has all been used.

13 When the dough is no longer sticky, continue mixing it with your fingers for 10 minutes more, until it looks shiny and feels elastic.

14 Using a pastry brush, evenly coat the inside of a large bowl with one tablespoon (15 ml) of butter.

15 Place the dough ball in the bowl and roll it around the bowl until its entire surface is buttered.

16 Cover the bowl with a kitchen towel and let it sit on the counter for 1½ hours, or until the dough doubles in size.

17 Use a pastry brush to butter a large baking sheet with one tablespoon (15 ml) of butter.

18 Again, lightly flour your countertop or pastry board. Turn the double-size dough out onto the floured surface.

19 With your fist, punch the dough down hard, then sprinkle it with the cinnamon.

20 Pat the dough down with your fingers and shape it into a twisted round shape. Grab the dough at each end, pulling and twisting it at the same time.

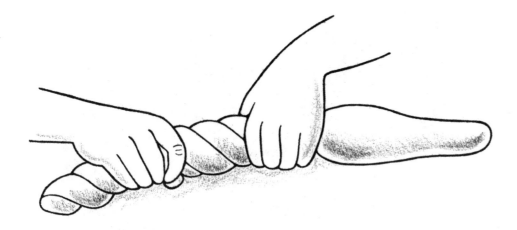

21 Place the dough on the buttered baking sheet. Pinch the ends of the dough together to form a circle.

22 Cover the dough with the kitchen towel and let it sit on the counter for 45 minutes, or until the circle of dough doubles in size.

23 Preheat the oven to 375°F (191°C)

24 After the dough has doubled, with a pastry brush, apply the egg and milk mixture to the top and sides of the dough.

25 Have an adult helper put the cake in the oven. Bake the cake until it's golden brown on top, about 25–35 minutes.

26 When the cake is done, have an adult helper remove it from the oven. Let the cake cool.

27 Push the plastic baby doll inside the cake.

Prepare the colored cake sugars and the icing:

28 Squeeze a dot of green pastry paste in the palm of your hand. Sprinkle 2 tablespoons (30 ml) sugar over the paste and rub the mixture together quickly in your hands. Repeat.

29 Place the green sugar on a sheet of wax paper and set aside. Wash your hands.

30 Repeat steps 28 and 29 with the purple, then yellow, pastry paste.

31 In a medium bowl, combine the powdered sugar, lemon juice, and 3 tablespoons (45 ml) water. Mix until smooth. If the icing is too stiff to spread, add the remaining water a tablespoon at a time until it's spreadable.

32 Spread the icing over the cake with a spatula.

33 From the top of the cake to its bottom, sprinkle a large stripe of green colored sugar on the cake. Repeat with the purple and yellow sugars.

34 Keep making rows of stripes on the king cake until all the sugar is used up, or the cake is covered with stripes of colored sugar.

35 Serve slices of king cake to your friends and have a great Mardi Gras.

Giving Thanks

Celebrating the harvest dates back to ancient times. Ceremonies, feasts, and offerings of foods to the gods were traditional ways in which people could express their gratitude. People thanked whatever gods they believed in for a good harvest because everyone would now have plenty of food on their table for the winter.

Today some societies continue to pay homage to spirits that they believe are responsible for blessing them with a good harvest. Others thank an individual god, not only for the food they've eaten, but also for all the other blessings they've received over the past year. But no matter how we express our thanks, everyone celebrates the harvest by enjoying a great feast with friends and family, and sharing some of their happiness and good fortune with others who don't have as much to be thankful for.

Pongal

Pongal is a three-day festival of thanksgiving for the rice and sugarcane crop that is celebrated in mid-January by the Hindus in southeast India. *Pongal* (pronounced pon-GAHL) is also the name of the sweet rice pudding prepared especially for the festival. During Pongal, Hindus give thanks to the sun god (Surya) and the rain god (Indra) who have blessed them with a plentiful harvest, especially of rice and sugarcane, which are important crops. They thank the cows, too, because they help plow the fields to plant the crops. Cows are always treated very well in India, and they are considered sacred animals.

65

During Pongal, Hindus also exchange colorful greeting cards with family, friends, and neighbors, and many visit relatives and friends in other villages to wish them a good harvest for the coming year. Women may give one another a gift of *jaggery*, a brown sugar made from palm sap.

Bhogi Pongal

The Hindus celebrate Pongal over three days. The first day of the celebration is called Bhogi Pongal. Families prepare for the holiday and the visit from the gods by cleaning their

Shiva, the god of the seasons, is one of the most popular gods in the Hindu religion.

Who Are the Hindus?

Hinduism is one of the oldest religions in the world and is practiced by over 700 million people. Most Hindus live in India, but they do not use the term "Hindu" to describe their religion. They call it *Sanatana dharma*, which means the eternal religion or eternal teaching.

There are no set rules in practicing Hinduism, but all Hindus share important beliefs. They believe that a supreme being, *Brahma*, a shapeless spirit, lives in everything. Hindus believe that in order to live a good life and reach *moshka*, salvation, you must either pray, study, and teach Hindu religion, treat others well every day of your life, or practice yoga and meditate.

The Hindu religion has thousands of gods and goddesses, in addition to Brahma, and each is responsible for something specific. For example, *Vishnu* is the protector of the universe, and *Shiva* controls day and night, the seasons, and birth and death. Brahma, Vishnu, and Shiva are the main gods in the Hindu religion.

houses from top to bottom. They coat their homes with fresh layers of terra-cotta clays or whitewash. They gather old junk from the house that has accumulated over the past year and burn it in a bonfire to symbolize the destruction of evil. After the cleaning ritual is completed, the Hindus use colored rice flour and water to paint beautiful designs, called *kilars,* on their walls or floors. The special patterns are signs of welcome to the gods.

The Hindus paint *kilars,* decorative colored patterns, on their homes to welcome the gods.

Surya Pongal

On the second day of the celebration, Surya Pongal, the Hindus cook up a feast, including the traditional sweet rice dish *pongal.* Many Hindus are vegetarians because they do not believe in killing animals. They believe that all living creatures are sacred. A typical festival meal, therefore, would include a variety of highly spiced vegetable dishes, lentils, plenty of rice, flatbreads such as *naan* and *chapati,* and yogurt. There would also be tea, water, or a refreshing yogurt drink called *lassi* to drink. For dessert, in addition to the *pongal,* there would be a variety of sweets and candies.

PONGAL FEAST

To make *pongal,* freshly harvested rice, brown sugar, and milk are put into a pot and boiled. When the mixture begins to bubble over, Hindus shout, *"Pongalo! Pongal!" Pongalo* means "to overflow." The bubbling over of the *pongal* is a symbol of abundance and prosperity, a gift from the gods of the sun and rain. The Hindus pray to Surya and offer the rice dish up to the god to thank him for a good harvest, then the families eat the *pongal.* Try making a pot of *pongal* for your family and then giving thanks for the food you eat. (Makes 4 servings.)

Here's What You Need

Ingredients

- [ ] ¹/₂ cup (119 ml) long-grain white rice
- [ ] 4 cups (948 ml) milk
- [ ] ¹/₂ cup (119 ml) brown sugar
- [ ] 1 teaspoon (5 ml) cardamom powder or 2 to 3 cardamom pods
- [ ] a handful of cashews or almonds (optional)
- [ ] raisins (optional)

Equipment

- [ ] measuring cups and spoons
- [ ] mixing bowl and spoon
- [ ] medium-size saucepan

Here's What You Do

1 Soak the rice in a bowl or pot for an hour.

2 Drain the rice, and set it aside.

3 Put the milk in the saucepan and heat until boiling.

4 Add the rice and sugar to the milk and turn the heat down to simmer.

5 Cook the rice mixture under a low heat until the rice is done and the mixture becomes thick.

6 Add the cardamom powder or pods and stir.

7 Add the nuts and raisins, if you'd like.

8 Serve the sweet *pongal* hot in bowls.

Mattu Pongal

On the third day of the feast, Mattu Pongal, the Hindus thank the cows for all their hard work of plowing the fields. The Hindus round up all of the cows, bulls, oxen, and water buffaloes to bathe and pretty them up. They decorate the animals with garlands of flowers and bells or leaves. Their horns are painted a bright color such as blue, yellow, or green. Sometimes silver bracelets are placed around the animals' ankles. The Hindus feed them sweets, such as fruits or raisins, then parade them around the village.

PET GARLAND

If you have a pet, why not make a garland of bells for it to thank it for its love and for being your friend. If you don't have a pet, you can wear the garland yourself or hang it as a decoration in your room.

Here's What You Need

- soutache (any color and width) *
- red, silver, blue or gold bells (small to medium)

*Soutache is a silky yarn that comes in many colors and sizes and is found in crafts stores

Here's What You Do

1 Measure your pet's neck with the soutache. Make sure it's long enough to fit over your pet's head and loose enough to be comfortable and not choke your pet.

2 Add the bells one at a time until the strand of soutache is filled with bells.

3 Tie the ends of the soutache in a double knot.

4 Hang the bell garland around your pet's neck.

Iriji

One of the most important celebrations in Nigeria, a nation of western Africa, is the harvest celebration, called *Iriji,* the New Yam Festival. (Yams are similar to sweet potatoes, but sweet potatoes only grow in the United States.) A group of people who live in west Africa called the *Igbos* (or Ibos) celebrate the yam because it is an important food. A plentiful yam harvest means that a whole community will eat well until the next harvest the following year. At harvesttime, the Igbos give thanks to the ancient gods for their good fortune.

There are many different Igbo groups and communities in Nigeria, and each community celebrates Iriji in a different way and at a different time of the year. Most festivals occur between July and September. An Igbo festival may be celebrated by traditional dances, songs, drumming, masquerades, wrestling, and a large feast featuring the newly harvested yams.

New Yam Celebration

In the Nkalagu village of Anambra, in June, the Igbos make many preparations for their New Yam Festival, which lasts for two days. By tradition, no one is allowed to eat the new yams before a yam ceremony.

On the first morning of the celebration, families make an altar in honor of their ancestors, the earth god *Ala,* and *Ihejioku*, the yam god. The village men then go out to their farms and dig up new yams. Farmers carry the yams back to their village, where they gather in the village square to sing a song of thanks to the earth and yam gods for a plentiful harvest that year and in the future.

The farmers return to their homes, where they make an offering to the gods and their ancestors. They offer the new yams, some white chalk, and a fowl. The family gathers in

Who Are the Igbos?

The Igbos have been living in west Africa for over 6,000 years. For most of this time, they lived peacefully as farmers and traders. Beginning in the sixteenth century, however, slave traders arrived in Africa, and hundreds of thousands of Igbos were sold to the Americas. Then in the 1800s the British tried to colonize Nigeria. The Africans continually fought them, and in the 1960s, Nigeria finally gained its independence from the British. Then a civil war broke out between the three main ethnic groups in Nigeria: the Igbo, Yoruba, and Hausa. By 1967, the Igbos had split from Nigeria to form their own state, the Republic of Biafra. Today the Igbos are again a part of Nigeria and live peacefully in villages of the Igbo states of Imo, Abia, Enugu, Anambra, Delta, Ebonyi, and Rivers. The social and cultural practices of the Igbos in these states vary widely. While the Igbos have adopted the Christian and Muslim religions, many continue to practice ancient religious traditions like the New Yam Festival.

front of an altar they prepared, and the Igbo father asks the spirits to accept his offerings and to bless his family with a good life, health, and plentiful yam harvests. The father slaughters the fowl, then chews some chalk and "blesses" the yams by spitting on not only the yams but also on his hands and the hands of the rest of the family. The chalk is used because it symbolizes purity and well-being.

Many Igbos save the blessed yams until the next year. Traditionally, the yams are tied around the *ogirishi,* a sacred tree that is said to bestow fertility. The tree becomes a symbol of the yam spirit. The Igbos believe the yam spirit lives inside of the yams and that this spirit will protect next year's harvest. Following the ceremony, the Igbos celebrate the festival by feasting with their family, friends, and neighbors.

Altarpieces symbolize the family and the yam god, who the Igbos worship before yam eating begins.

Igbo Gods

While millions of Igbos today are Christians or Muslims, many still pray to the ancient Igbo gods. In the Igbo religion, all objects in nature, such as trees, farms, fields, mountains, are believed to be given life by the spirits who live inside them. The Igbos believe that if they honor the spirits who live inside a natural object, such as the yam, they will be rewarded with a good harvest. If the Igbos neglect the yam spirits, they believe the crop will be bad. Ala, the earth goddess, is the mother of the Igbo people and the symbol of life. Her husband, *Ndiche,* is their ancestors' forefather. Because the Igbos plant many crops on Ala's land, they pray to her and the gods who will help the crops grow. *Igwe* is a water god who provides welcomed rains to the crop, while Ndiche enriches the soil that will produce good and plentiful harvests. The Igbos believe that these three gods are essential in providing food for their communities.

Feasting, Wrestling, and Dancing

On the second day of the yam festival, the villagers gather to watch young men participate in wrestling contests. In the morning, the wrestlers eat roasted yams, which they believe will give them strength against their opponents. In the afternoon the village community gathers in the village square. They celebrate the day by eating, drinking, and talking with their neighbors, family, and friends, while watching the competition. Village elders are chosen as judges.

The Igbo wrestlers, split into two fighting teams, are welcomed into the village square by the sounds of the village drummers. The villagers gather in a circle around the wrestlers to watch the competition. When a wrestler wins, drummers beat their drums and young women celebrate the victory by coming into the circle and dancing. The wrestlers do not win any prizes, but they are admired and respected by their village. The yam festival ends in the evening, when the wrestling matches are over.

IGBO DRUM

Drums are a very important instrument in Africa. They are played on both sad and joyful occasions, and they are always played at some point during harvest festivals. The Igbos play a variety of drums, such as one made from the calabash, a large bottle-shaped gourd. To create an instrument, the Igbos

Igbo Masquerades

In some Igbo communities, villagers masquerade and perform beautiful choreographed dances. Large, detailed masks are made from a variety of materials. Some are carved from wood, while others are made from bark, animal skins, plant fibers, and woven cloth. During the New Yam Festival, masked and costumed men gather in the village square. The community's male elders, village leaders, and younger male dancers participate in the masquerade. Traditionally, women are not allowed to masquerade. The drums beat and the Igbos perform ritual harvest dances. The Igbos believe that the masqueraders embody the spirit of the harvest gods. So through the masqueraders the gods are then able to interact with the community.

cut the gourd horizontally to form a large bowl. The drum, decorated with designs etched on its surface, is played upside down, struck with bundles of thin, flexible sticks. The *udu,* an Igbo pot drum, is a large bottle-shaped clay pot with an opening at its top and a hole in its side. The drum is played by covering the side hole with the palm of one hand while hitting the top hole of the drum with the other hand. By covering and hitting the drum's openings in a variety of ways the drummer can produce different tones from the instrument. The *udu* can also be played by striking the drum with your fingers. Other drums used by the Igbos are the slit drum, a narrow rectangular wooden drum with a long slit at its top, which is banged on both sides with two large sticks, and cylindrical and rectangular drums that are covered with animal skin and decorated with plant fibers and cowrie shells. Try making your own drum from stuff you find around the house. Then add traditional African decorations, such as wooden beads and cowrie shells.

Here's What You Need

- [ ] empty paint can, with handle removed, or an empty coffee can
- [ ] can opener
- [ ] roll of twine
- [ ] 16-by-20 inches (41-by-51 cm) canvas sheet (available at an art supply shop)
- [ ] scissors
- [ ] cardboard
- [ ] glue
- [ ] medium to large rubber or elastic bands (available at an art supply or crafts shop)
- [ ] materials for decorating your drum: cowrie shells or African beads (available at crafts stores or bead shops)

Igbo drums

Here's What You Do

1 Take the bottom of the can off with the can opener. Discard it. Make sure there are no sharp pieces of metal poking out of the can.

2 Take your twine and thread it through the opening of the can, down the outside of the can, then again through the inside. Tie the twine into a tight double knot. Make sure the knot remains on the inside of the can.

3 Continue threading the twine through the opening and around the sides of the can until the can is completely covered. Cut the twine, and on the inside of the can tie a double knot in the end.

4 Measure a piece of canvas to fit over the can's mouth with about 1 inch (2.5 cm) extra all around. Cut out the canvas circle.

5 Trace the diameter of the can's mouth on a piece of cardboard. Cut out the circle.

6 Glue the cardboard onto the center of the canvas. Let the glue dry.

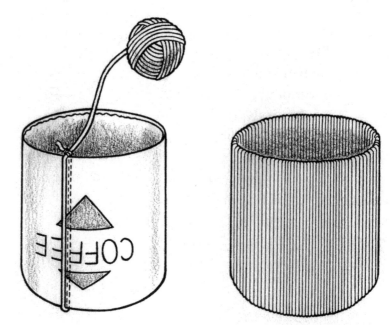

7 Place the canvas over the can, making sure the cardboard circle is aligned with the can's mouth. The canvas will overlap about an inch or more from the lip of the can.

8 Use a rubber band to secure the canvas to the top of the can.

9 Take one of the elastic bands and measure it to make sure that it fits somewhat loosely around the can. Cut it.

10 String your beads and/or cowrie shells onto the rubber band. Take the two ends of the band and tie them into a double knot. Slip the band over the can's mouth. Remove the rubber band.

11 Repeat steps 9 and 10 twice more to make two more beaded bands for your drum.

12 Play your drum with your hands or a wooden spoon.

Yam Feast

There are many types of African yams, but none resemble the orange sweet potatoes that are grown in America. African yams do taste sweet, but they are white on the inside. Because the yam is a very versatile vegetable, the Igbos can prepare it in many different ways. Yams are roasted, boiled, added to soups and stews, french fried, mashed to make a traditional dish called *fufu*, or dried and ground to make flour. The Igbos might serve the yams with fish, chicken or lamb, and vegetables such as oil bean, *uku*, a type of pumpkin, corn, a variety of African greens, and a pepper soup made up of chicken, beef, or lamb, pepper and vegetables. Dessert might be mangoes, guavas, pineapple, or citrus fruits. Drink would include palm wine, beer, and fruit juices.

Igbo drum

Fufu

Celebrate the Igbo New Yam Festival as the Igbos do by eating a yam dish. While the Igbos use modern utensils, many still like eating their meals in the traditional way—with their hands. Serve the *fufu* as a side dish with your dinner. (Makes 4–5 servings.)

Here's What You Need

Ingredients
- [ ] 4 small- to medium-size yams
- [ ] ½ stick (4 tablespoons) (60 ml) butter or margarine, softened

Equipment
- [ ] large pot
- [ ] mixing bowl
- [ ] potato masher or fork
- [ ] adult helper

Here's What You Do

1 Rinse the yams in warm water.

2 Place the yams in a large pot and cover them with water.

3 Have your adult helper boil the yams over low-medium heat for 30 to 40 minutes, or until a knife easily pierces the yams.

4 Have your adult helper remove and drain the yams. Let them cool a bit until you can handle them with your hands.

5 Peel the yams and put them into a large bowl. Add the butter.

6 Mash the yams and butter together with a large fork or potato masher. The *fufu* will be very thick. Serve warm.

Crop-Over

-BARBADOS-

In early July, Barbadians, who are natives of Barbados (pronounced Bar-BAY-dos), an island in the British West Indies, celebrate the harvest of the sweetest crop in the world— sugarcane. The national harvest festival is called Crop-Over. It dates back to the 1800s, when the slaves who worked on the sugarcane plantations celebrated the end of the sugarcane crop harvest, which was usually long and hard. The Barbadians take part in many of the rituals their ancestors did while also celebrating in some new ways. During Crop-Over you can see parades, dances, and fireworks, hear calypso bands, enjoy arts and crafts, and taste the same kind of food and drinks that the slaves prepared in the nineteenth century. Crop-Over is a three-week-long festival of feasting and enjoying the island's many treasures.

Festival Fun

Today, the Barbadians celebrate the end of the cane season by holding a parade of flower-decorated carts to recall the work their ancestors did. This grand procession marks the beginning of the Crop-Over festivities.

For three weeks, each Barbadian *parish,* or city, holds its own fairs and festivities, which might include a donkey derby, a goat race, or contests to see who can catch a greased pig, drink the most coconut milk, or cut the most sugarcane. All around the island there are also calypso and steel pan music competitions and live concerts. Calypsos are songs that usually satirize local events or famous people. A steel pan or drum, created in Trinidad, which is also in the Caribbean, is an instrument made from an oil drum and played with wooden sticks. During the festival there are also lively matches of stick lickey, a sport similar to fencing.

Many decorative Barbadian arts and crafts are sold during the festival. The islanders are known for their beautiful wooden sculptures, woven straw mats, and colorful clay pottery.

The First Crop-Over

In the 1600s over 10 million slaves were brought from Africa to the Caribbean. Many of these slaves ended up working long hours planting, caring for, and harvesting sugarcane, a tall grass. At harvesttime, the sugarcane had to be cut and made into sugar within two days or the sugar inside the cane would spoil. To do this, the slaves put the cane stalks in a huge iron press that the slaves would turn to squeeze out the juice. The cane juice was then boiled in large kettles. When the juice evaporated, thick molasses and sugar crystals were left at the bottom of the pot. The slaves poured the molasses and the sugar into separate kegs and drove them in donkey carts to the seaport, where they would be taken by ship to be sold in Europe and North America.

When the last of the sugarcane harvest was loaded up onto the carts, the slaves would shout "Crop over!" to let the others know that their hard work was done. The slaves celebrated by feasting and dancing to the sounds of handmade instruments on the plantation fields.

CLAY POT

To celebrate the sugarcane harvest, try making a clay pot similar to the ones the slaves used to store cane sugar. You can make your pot any size you like. While Barbadian pottery is always beautiful and colorful, there aren't any traditional letterings or designs used to make the work. The potters just let their imaginations run wild.

Here's What You Need

- ☐ 10–12 pounds (4½–5½ kg) self-hardening or wet-set clay
- ☐ wooden board
- ☐ tape measure or ruler
- ☐ acrylic paints (choose sunny island colors, such as light blues, yellows, greens, pinks, and oranges)
- ☐ paintbrushes

Here's What You Do

1 Tear the block of clay in half and soften it by pulling it apart and pushing it back together, pulling it with your fingers until it feels soft and pliable.

2 Tear off a piece of clay the size of a Ping-Pong ball.

3 Roll the clay between the palms of your hands until it's about the length and thickness of a carrot.

4 Lay the clay on the board. Roll the clay back and forth until it resembles a long snake measuring 6 to 8 inches (15 to 20 cm) long and about the width of your pinky.

5 Continue making clay snakes until you have about 10. Now you can begin making the bottom of your pot.

6 Lay one clay snake on the wooden board and wrap it around itself again and again until it looks like a coil. Leave about ½ inch (1 cm) left uncoiled.

7 Pick up your next clay snake and join it to the end of the one on your table by gently pushing the ends into each other.

8 Continue connecting the snakes to make the bottom for your pot until it's the size that you want.

9 Smooth the end of the last snake into the pot's bottom with your finger.

10 Smooth out the base by running your fingertips across the coils, from the outside to the middle. Working clockwise, continue smoothing the coils. If a lump appears in the middle of the base, push it down with your fingers and smooth it out.

11 Begin to make the sides of the pot by aligning a clay snake around the edges of the pot's base. If you run out of clay, repeat steps 1 through 4.

12 When you have a circle of clay on top of the pot's base, join the side and bottom of the pot together by smoothing your fingers across its seam, which is the point where both pieces of clay meet.

13 Continue building your pot with clay snakes until it's the height you want. Let the pot fully dry.

14 To make a lid for your pot, measure the width of your pot with a tape measure or ruler. Soften up your clay, then make some more clay snakes.

15 Lay a clay snake on the wooden board and wrap it around itself like a coil. Continue building the pot's lid until it measures the width of your pot.

16 Smooth out the clay coils, as in step 10.

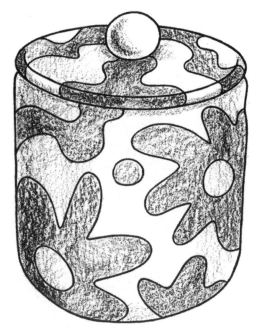

17 To make a pot handle, roll a piece of clay into a small ball the size of a Ping-Pong ball. Place it onto the center of the lid and join it to the lid by smoothing the clay together with your fingers.

18 Let the lid dry.

19 Give your pot some Barbadian flavor by painting it with some sunny island colors, such as yellow, sky blue, green, or pink.

Kadooment Day

On the final day of Crop-Over, which is the first Monday in August, Barbadians celebrate Grand Kadooment Day, a public holiday. *Kadooment* (pronounced Ka-DOO-ment) is a word that means "party." Grand Kadooment is the final and largest party of the festival. On this day there is a huge carnival-like parade, and a contest among costumed bands takes place. Twenty-five costumed bands compete in the national stadium in Bridgetown, the capital of Barbados. As calypso music blasts, the bands parade and dance across the stadium. A panel of judges decides which band has the best costumes in Barbados. The judges also choose the king and queen of the crop.

Mr. Harding, a reminder of hard times on the sugar plantation, is set on fire during Crop-Over.

Mr. Harding

Following the costume competitions at the national stadium, costumed bands, calypso bands, and parade goers march for five miles to the Garrison Savannah, the Bridgetown town square, where the final celebration of Crop-Over takes place. Carried to the procession is a life-size doll that represents a ruthless plantation owner named Mr. Harding. The doll is stuffed with rags, straw, or sugarcane debris and is a symbol of the cruel treatment slaves endured on the sugarcane plantation. When they reach the Garrison Savannah, the Barbadians set the doll on fire, then pelt the figure with stones. After Mr. Harding is no more, the people set off firecrackers, sing, and dance into the night.

Crop-Over Feast

The Barbadians do not make any special dishes for the three-week-long Crop-Over Festival, they just enjoy the many delicious foods already available on the island. One obvious treat to enjoy during the festival is sugarcane juice. Barbadians press the juice out of the canes to produce a sweet and refreshing drink. Besides sugarcane juice, there's coconut milk, ginger beer, *sorrel,* which is a sweet drink made from a red-flowering plant that belongs to the hibiscus family, and rum punch, a favorite Caribbean drink. To eat, you will find *roti,* a kind of West Indian burrito that's filled with curried chicken, beef, or vegetables and encased in a flat dough; flying-fish sandwiches with fries and coleslaw; *cutters,* rolls stuffed with meat or cheese fillings, coconut bread, *cou-cou,* which is cornmeal and okra pudding, and curry dishes.

GINGER BEER

If you're a fan of ginger, you'll enjoy a tall, cool glass of ginger beer. It's not really beer, of course, but it has more kick than regular ginger ale. In Barbados, the fizzy bottled drink is sold by street vendors all over the island, but many locals enjoy making their own ginger beer. Try making some yourself. (Makes 4 servings.)

Here's What You Need

Ingredients

- ¼ cup (59 ml) fresh ginger, peeled and grated
- ¾ cup (178 ml) sugar
- 4 cups (948 ml) water
- juice from ½ of one lime

Equipment

- measuring cup
- 2 large pitchers
- adult helper

Here's What You Do

1 Ask your adult helper to peel and grate the ginger.

2 Into a large pitcher, add the ginger, sugar, water, and lime juice. Stir.

3 Let the ginger mixture sit at room temperature on a counter for 24 hours.

4 The next day, use a sieve, or strainer, and strain the ginger beer into another large pitcher.

5 Put the pitcher of ginger beer in the refrigerator until chilled.

6 Serve in tall glasses over ice.

Thanksgiving

—THE UNITED STATES—

America's traditional harvest feast is called Thanksgiving and is celebrated on the fourth Thursday of November. Although in modern times most Americans aren't involved in actual harvests, they still give thanks for the food they eat. They also use the occasion as a time to express thanks for their family, friends, and all the good things that have happened to them over the past year. People travel near and far to celebrate the feast with their relatives and friends. Everyone looks forward to the traditional turkey dinner that is served on this holiday.

At Thanksgiving, Americans also remember others who may not be as fortunate as themselves. Many people donate goods through their churches or charities so that others will have hot food and warm clothes for the winter.

Who Were the Pilgrims?

In England in the 1600s, a group of Christians called Separatists left England because they did not agree with the Church of England. In 1620 they received permission to help settle a colony in the New World. On September 16, 1620, 102 Separatists—soldiers, servants, and laborers—sailed aboard the *Mayflower* from Plymouth, England, to try to reach Virginia. The passengers became known as Pilgrims, because a pilgrim is someone who travels far away from home for religious reasons. Sixty-six days later, the Pilgrims landed near Cape Cod, Massachusetts. The Pilgrims explored the land and decided to settle in Plimoth, which the explorer John Smith had named years before.

The First Harvest Festival

The first British settlers in Massachusetts, the Pilgrims, arrived just before winter, so food was scarce. By spring of the following year, 57 Pilgrims had died. Luckily, a Wampanoag Indian, Tisquantum (Squanto), offered them help. Squanto was an ex-slave who had learned English. He taught the settlers how to fish, hunt deer and turkey, and grow native vegetables, such as pumpkins, Indian corn, and squash. Without the help of Squanto and other Native Americans, the Pilgrims probably would not have survived another winter. In the fall of 1621, the Pilgrims had harvested plenty of food, and they were very thankful. To celebrate, Governor Bradford decided to have a three-day feast. The Pilgrims invited their new friends, but they were surprised when Chief Massasoit showed up with over 90 braves. The Wampanoag brought an offering of five deer for the feast, which also included wild turkey, geese, fish, and plenty of vegetables, such as pumpkins and corn, and fruit. The Pilgrims and the Wampanoag played games, held foot races and jumping contests, and showed off their skills with rifles and bows and arrows.

Modern Thanksgiving

Today Americans celebrate Thanksgiving much like the Pilgrims did, by sitting down with family and friends to share many of the same vegetables and meats that the Wampanoags taught the Pilgrims to farm or hunt. It is traditional to cook a roasted turkey stuffed with a mixture of bread or wild rice and foods like chestnuts, oysters, and sausages. Side dishes include cranberry sauce, candied sweet potatoes, mashed potatoes, squash, and corn. For dessert, there is usually a selection of pies, such as apple, sweet potato, and pumpkin.

Pumpkin Pie

The Pilgrims always had plenty of pumpkins to eat. Pumpkins were easy to grow, even in the rocky soil of Massachusetts. The Pilgrims most likely ate boiled chunks of pumpkin or mashed them to make a thick pudding or a tasty soup. Because the Pilgrims lacked flour and sugar, they probably didn't turn out a tasty pumpkin pie, but modern-day families enjoy creating this delicious and easy-to-make dessert for their families and friends. Here's a traditional recipe to try for the holiday.

Here's What You Need

Ingredients

- [ ] 1 15-ounce (425-g) can pumpkin puree
- [ ] 1 14-ounce (400-g) can sweetened condensed milk
- [ ] 2 eggs
- [ ] 1 teaspoon (5 ml) cinnamon
- [ ] ¼ (1.25 ml) teaspoon ginger
- [ ] ¼ teaspoon (1.25 ml) nutmeg
- [ ] a dash of salt
- [ ] 1 9-inch (23-cm) pie shell, unbaked
- [ ] vanilla ice cream or whipped cream, optional

Equipment

- [ ] mixing bowl and spoon
- [ ] measuring spoons
- [ ] oven mitt
- [ ] adult helper

Here's What You Do

1 Preheat the oven to 425°F (220°C).

2 In a large bowl, mix together the pumpkin, condensed milk, eggs, and spices.

3 Pour the pie filling into the pie shell.

4 Ask an adult helper to put the pie in the oven. Bake the pie for 15 minutes then reduce the oven temperature to 350°F (180°C).

5 Continue baking the pie for 35 to 40 more minutes, or until a knife inserted into the center of the pie comes out clean.

6 Ask your adult helper to remove the pie from the oven when it's done.

7 Serve the pie warm with a dollop of vanilla ice cream or whipped cream on the side.

Thanksgiving Becomes Official

The first official Thanksgiving holiday was declared on December 18, 1777, during the American Revolution. Thirteen states celebrated that feast. But it wasn't until Abraham Lincoln became president that Thanksgiving Day became a national holiday. Sarah Bush Hale, a writer who wrote about Thanksgiving for women's magazines, helped. Thanksgiving was Hale's favorite holiday; she wrote letters that convinced the president how important and meaningful the celebration was. The date would change again, but in December 1941, Congress set a permanent date for the holiday—the fourth Thursday in November.

parade of marching bands, giant balloons of cartoon characters and superheroes, floats, and celebrities. Millions of people line the parade route or watch on TV every year.

And like the Pilgrims and Wampanoag Indians, Americans also celebrate the holiday by playing games. Football games are now a part of the American Thanksgiving tradition. While getting ready for the big feast, many families gather to watch professional football teams on TV.

Thanksgiving Day Parade and Football

As the popularity of Thanksgiving grew, Americans created new traditions, the most exciting of which is the Thanksgiving Day parade. The first parade was organized in 1920 by a department store in Pennsylvania. In 1924, Macy's department store held its first parade in New York City. Today, Macy's is known worldwide for its festive

Thanksgiving Day parades are festive traditions in New York and Philadelphia.

Thanksgiving Symbols

Traditional Thanksgiving decorations are often symbols of the harvest festival. Many people decorate their homes with Indian corn, a multicolored corn with kernels whose color ranges from white to black to deep red. The corn originated in Central and South America, where it was grown by the native peoples. During the holiday you'll also see pictures of Pilgrims, Native Americans, corn dollies, and wild turkeys decorating classrooms and shops. Sometimes people gather the types of fruits and vegetables that the Wampanoags helped the Pilgrims farm and put them in a basket or cornucopia (a horn of plenty) centerpiece. This symbolizes the plentiful harvest. Others fill pumpkin shells or gourds with winter flower bouquets.

Pilgrim Corn Dolly

Back in the colonial days, children didn't have many toys. But they learned from their Native American neighbors how to make a corn doll. These dolls, made from corn husks and silk, are a symbol of the Thanksgiving harvest. Make a corn dolly, or two, to add to your traditional Thanksgiving decorations.

Here's What You Need

- 50 dried corn husks (found in crafts stores, or look for tamale wrappers at a Mexican grocery)
- pan filled with water
- 5 pipe cleaners
- cotton balls
- markers or paint and brush
- corn silk or yarn
- glue

Here's What You Do

1 Soak the husks in water for about five minutes to soften them up.

2 Tear two husks into narrow strips to be used later for tying bundles of husks together.

3 Take a husk and lay it flat on your work space.

4 Roll one or two more pieces of husks into a ball and place it in the middle of the strip on your work space. Bring the two far ends of the flat husk together.

5 Twist the pipe cleaner around the bottom of the ball to make the head of the dolly.

6 To make the arms, first roll a husk around a pipe cleaner, then roll another piece of husk around it.

7 Tie husk strips about 1/2 inch (1 cm) from each end of the husk roll to make a wrist and hand.

8 Insert the arms between the husks under the dolly's neck.

9 Stick one or two cotton balls under the arms to make a torso, then tie the sheets of husks together with one or two husk strips.

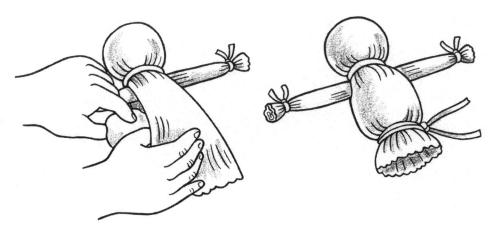

10 Take 10 to 15 husks and lay them under and around the dolly, covering its body (but not its head) completely. The dolly should look as if it's wearing an upside-down skirt.

11 Use husk strips to tie the husks together about ½ inch (1cm) above the dolly's waist.

12 Fold the husks down. Now you have a skirt.

13 To make a boy dolly, split the skirt husks into two bundles and tie them at the knees and the ankles.

14 Draw a face on your corn dolly.

15 To make hair, glue strands of corn silk on top of the doll's head, or glue on pieces of yarn.

Renewing the Spirit

Many societies celebrate holidays that honor their ancestors, their spiritual beliefs, and/or their spiritual leaders. These special festivals are a time when people can reaffirm their faith in their gods, themselves, and others. It is a time to look inside yourself and think of ways in which you can be a better person, and to think about and celebrate the things that are important in life. It's also a time to honor the struggles and sacrifices of people in the past that have made life on this earth better for everyone.

El Día de los Reyes

For Christians in Latin America, January 6 has a very special meaning. It is thought to be the day when the three kings, or three wise men, arrived in Bethlehem to give gifts to the newborn Jesus. *El Día de los Reyes* (pronounced el DEE-a day lohs RAY-yes) (Three Kings Day) is a time for great celebration. In Mexico, as in other Latin American countries, families go to mass, and kids, family, and friends exchange gifts, eat traditional Mexican foods, and stuff themselves with cake, candies, and cookies. Every year there are *fiestas* (parties) and activities for children all over Mexico.

The Legend of the Three Kings

It is said that the tradition of giving gifts during the Christmas season can be traced back to the three kings: Gaspar, king of Tarsus; Melchior, king of Arabia; and Balthasar, king of Sheba. According to the legend, the three kings were traveling to Bethlehem from different parts of the world to see the Christ Child. Each was guided by a blazing star that appeared in the sky. Eventually the kings met one another in Bethlehem, and they all found the baby Jesus together. The kings offered the baby special symbolic gifts: Melchior brought gold, Gaspar gave him frankincense, and Balthasar offered myrrh. The gold stands for tribute, frankincense for worship, and myrrh for death.

Dear Melchior, Gaspar and Balthasar...

For kids, Three Kings Day is especially sweet because they receive three gifts, one from each king. Weeks before the holiday, kids write letters to the three kings, just like kids in America write to Santa Claus, telling them how good they were during the year and what gifts they hope to receive. On the eve of Three Kings Day, the children leave the note inside one of their shoes and place the shoe near the doorway that the kings will enter. They also leave a glass of water and some grass for the kings' camels. In the morning, the water and grass have disappeared, and presents and sweets for the children have been placed near or inside the shoes.

Feasting

After opening presents, families attend a special mass for the holiday, then they return home to serve the *rosca de reyes,* three kings bread, which is similar to the king cake made for Mardi Gras. The bread is shaped like a crown, and studded with dried fruits. Inside the cake is a tiny plastic doll. The person who gets the slice of cake with the doll inside will have a good year. During the day, family and friends feast on tortillas filled with meats, *patacones* (a type of banana), *tamales* (seasoned ground meat rolled in cornmeal dough, wrapped in corn husks and steamed), *bolitos de coco* (coconut candies), and Mexican hot chocolate.

Hot Chocolate

Try making a warm mug of hot chocolate on a frosty night. (Makes 4 servings.)

Ingredients

☐ 4 cups (948 ml) milk

☐ 4 ounces (100 grams) sweetened chocolate, grated*

☐ ½ cinnamon stick

* Mexican or Spanish chocolate can be found in the Spanish foods section of your supermarket

Equipment

☐ 1 large saucepan

☐ 1 mixing spoon

☐ measuring cup and spoon

Here's What You Do

1 In a large saucepan, heat the milk, chocolate, and cinnamon, stirring until the chocolate dissolves.

2 Remove the pan from the heat.

3 Remove the stick of cinnamon, pour the hot chocolate into mugs, and enjoy with your friends.

Snapshots with the Kings

In downtown Mexico City, kids can get their pictures taken with the three kings, just as kids can have their pictures taken with Santa Claus. The kings, dressed in elaborate robes and turbans, sit on thrones while children hop into their laps for a holiday picture. Other cities hold parades or fiestas where there is dancing in the streets and bands playing until late at night. The three kings often make an appearance, riding on horseback.

Piñata Parties

At many fiestas, kids in Mexico play a game that centers around a *piñata,* a clay or papier-mâché container filled with candies and/or small toys. In the old days, the piñata was a religious symbol. The goodies inside the piñata were "temptations" from the devil. Today, the piñata is great fun anytime. Piñatas can be made into many fun shapes—from donkeys to stars to soccer balls—and they can be decorated any way you like.

The piñata is first hung above the children's heads. A child is blindfolded, handed a stick, and twirled around. The child gets a few tries to whack at the piñata, then another child gets a turn. Finally, it cracks open, and the toys and candies crash to the floor. The kids all dive to gather up as much as they can.

Kids thwack piñatas filled with goodies and toys to celebrate the holiday.

It's Piñata Time

Celebrate Three Kings Day by making your own festive piñata and having a piñata party

Here's What You Need

- several newspapers
- $\frac{1}{2}$ cup (118 ml) flour
- 1 teaspoon (5 ml) salt
- $\frac{1}{2}$ cup (118 ml) water
- measuring cup and spoon
- large bowl or small bucket
- balloon
- string
- scissors
- knife
- individually wrapped chocolate, hard candy, and gum to fill half of the balloon
- tissue or crepe paper (any color), acrylic paint, glitter, stick-on stars, etc.
- glue or glue stick

Here's What You Do

1 Tear the newspaper into strips and put them in a neat pile.

2 To make the papier-mâché paste, put $\frac{1}{2}$ cup (118 ml) flour and 1 teaspoon (5 ml) salt into a large bowl or small bucket. Slowly stir in the $\frac{1}{2}$ cup (118 ml) water.

3 Stir the mixture until it's thick and smooth.

4 Blow up a large balloon. Tie the balloon.

5 Dip a strip of newspaper into the paste. Remove the excess paste from the strip with your fingers.

6 Apply the first strip to the balloon horizontally. Continue pasting the strips horizontally on the balloon. At the top of the balloon, leave a nickel-size hole uncovered with paste.

7 After you've completed one entire layer of horizontal strips, apply another layer of papier-mâché strips to the balloon, this time laying the strips on vertically.

8 Add two more layers of papier-mâché, one horizontal and one vertical.

9 Let the papier-mâché dry completely. (It may take two days or more.)

10 Pop the balloon with a pin and shake out the balloon fragments.

11 Have an adult cut a 2-by-2-inch (5-by-5-cm) square into the papier-mâché balloon mold, starting at the hole. Keep the square that you cut out. The square should include the hole.

12 Ask an adult to punch a small hole on either side of the 2-inch square opening with a nail.

13 Thread the string through the holes on the piñata.

14 Decorate your piñata with paint, glitter, crepe paper, or tissue paper, etc.

15 Fill the piñata with your goodies and replace the square cutout.

16 Cover the square piece with decorations.

17 Grab the ends of the string and tie them together.

18 Have an adult hang up your piñata outdoors, or in a safe place at home.

19 To whack the piñata, use something like a plastic bat.

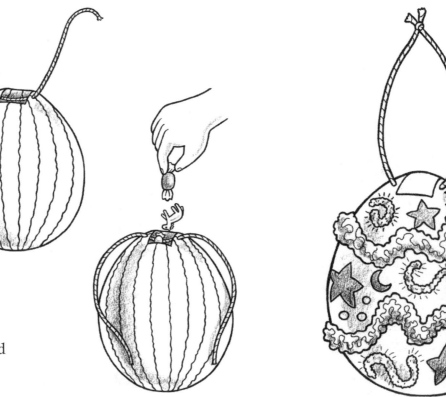

Obon

Obon (pronounced OH-bone) (also called Bon), the Festival of the Dead, is a three-day Buddhist celebration that is held from July 13 to 15 in Japan. (In Japanese-American communities, Buddhist temples hold weekend celebrations from July 13 to August 15.)

In Japan, Obon is a national holiday, and all businesses and schools are closed. Japanese Buddhists believe the souls of the dead return to their homes during this time to visit their relatives. For the festival, the Japanese who live away often return to their homes to visit, and clean and decorate the graves or tombs of their family. In Japan, Obon is one of the busiest travel days of the year. Obon is a time for the Japanese to remember the good deeds of their relatives. And if the relatives were not good on earth, it's a time to say prayers that may help the unseen spirits have a better afterlife. During Obon, it's also important to give to others. Families and friends often exchange presents during the holiday.

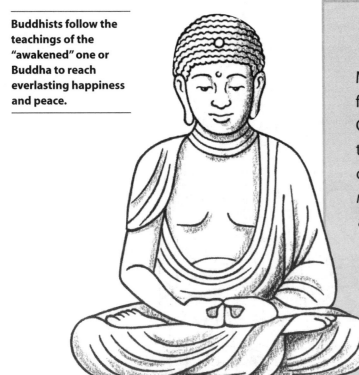

Buddhists follow the teachings of the "awakened" one or Buddha to reach everlasting happiness and peace.

Who Are the Buddhists?

More than 300 million people worldwide are Buddhists. They follow the teachings of the Buddha, who was born Siddhartha Gautama, in India in 563 B.C.E. Siddhartha was unhappy with all the pain and suffering in the world and he wondered what could be done to make everyone truly joyful. One day while *meditating* (thinking deeply), he became the Buddha, or "the awakened." He believed humans were unhappy because of their behavior and desire for material things. He wrote a series of laws, *dharma*, that humans could practice to become better people, such as being generous and mindful of others, and thinking positively. Those who followed the dharma correctly would eventually reach *nirvana*, a condition of everlasting peace and happiness.

Celebrating the Ancestors

To prepare for the festival, the Japanese visit the market to buy food and decorations. Families clean and decorate their homes and their ancestors' tombs with attractive plants and branches, incense, fruit, and *mochi* (rice balls).

On the first day of the Obon festival, families create altars or shrines in their homes to honor their relatives. Placed on the altar is a small meal for the spirits to eat. It includes foods they enjoyed while alive, including fruits, vegetables, and sweets. In the evening, the Japanese light lanterns and take a trip to their relatives' graves. Lanterns are left at the grave sites and hung outside of homes to help the ancestral spirits find their way and to welcome their arrival. Some families then light a small fire in front of their homes or in a fireplace, and talk to the spirits as if they were still alive. The next day, friends and family visit each other, pray, feast, and honor their ancestors' memory.

Families decorate ancestral grave sites with flowers, incense, and special foods.

PAPER LANTERNS

In the Buddhist religion, lanterns are a symbol of kindness to all living things. During the holiday, you'll find the round white lanterns, made of paper, hanging outside of homes, on grave sites, and as decorations for the community *Obon-odori,* which are Japanese folk dances. For this reason, some people refer to Obon as the Festival of Lanterns. To celebrate Obon, remember the spirit of your ancestors by making a lantern. Make lanterns in as many shapes as you wish.

Here's What You Need

- [ ] 1 sheet of 8½-by-11-inch (22-by-28-cm) construction paper, any color
- [ ] ruler
- [ ] scissors
- [ ] tape
- [ ] hole punch
- [ ] 12 inches (30 cm) string

Here's What You Do

1 Fold the paper horizontally from left to right; then fold in half again, folding from the top to bottom.

2 Holding the paper horizontally, fold the paper from left to right, then fold in half again from top to bottom.

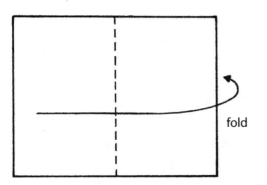

fold

3 With your scissors, snip out designs in the four edges of the paper.

4 Open up your paper. You now have two symmetrical patterns.

5 Bring the two 8½-inch (22-cm) sides together and tape along the edge.

6 Use your hole punch to punch a hole in the top of each side of the lantern

7 Thread a piece of string through the holes to make a handle for the lantern.

8 Tie a knot at the end of the string. Hang up your lantern.

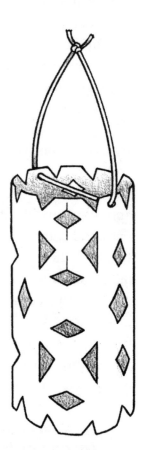

The Legend of Moggallana

During Obon, Buddhists tell the legend of a young boy, Moggallana, and his mother. Moggallana's mother wanted her son to have the best of everything and tried to acquire lots of material things for him. While she loved her son, she was not kind to others. Moggallana could see into the future, and he saw his mother living in a world of devils. She was very hungry and thirsty, so Moggallana took her some food. When his mother touched the food, it turned into fire because she did not think about sharing the food with the other hungry devils. Moggallana was sad and asked Buddha for help. The Buddha told him that his mother had committed many evil deeds, but if Moggallana made offerings to a group of monks, his mother might be saved. Buddha also said that Moggallana should ask the monks to perform a memorial service for his mother so she would be saved. Moggallana followed Buddha's advice, and the mother was released from the world of the devils and reborn into a beautiful and peaceful land. The son was so happy that he danced with joy, and all the monks joined him in the dance. It is said that this is how the Obon folk dance, Obon-odori, originated.

Folk Dancing and Singing

During the festival, the Japanese enjoy watching and participating in the Obon-odori, a traditional folk dance. With two large wooden sticks, a musician beats an enormous round double-sided drum called a *taiko.* The taiko drum was once used to call people to prayer at Buddhist temples. As the drum sounds, hundreds of women, men, boys, and girls form a circle around the drummer. They wear colorful traditional Japanese dress, such as *kimonos* and *yukatas.* A kimono, worn by men and women, is a loose-fitting robe with long wide sleeves and a sash that is tied at the waist. A yukata is a shorter and lighter version of the kimono. Many people also wear *geta,* platform sandals.

The dancers move around in a circle, making simple choreographed hand gestures and dance steps. They repeat these movements as they make their dance in a circle. There are several types of Obon-odori. Some dances include round bamboo fans that the dancers move gracefully through the air, while another dance may use a *kachi-kachi,* two sticks of bamboo that are hit together. The faster the drums beat, the quicker the dancers whirl as they move their feet and hands, or move their fans through the air.

Behind every Obon-odori is a tale that symbolizes the hard work that was done by their ancestors. The dance called the *Tanko Bushi,* or the Coal Miner's Dance, is about the hard work of a coal miner. With their hand movements, the dancers pretend to be doing the miner's work, digging the coal, heaving it, and wiping the sweat off their brows. Other tales include the rice farmer and the fisherman.

Obon Feast

The Japanese feast every day of the three-day festival. When grandparents, aunts, and a host of cousins arrive home for Obon, they can expect to sit down to feasts of rice balls, noodle soups, beef, fish, and vegetables. For dessert there is fruit or a layered rice cake.

Soba Noodle Soup

The Japanese have been eating noodles for over 2000 years. The long *soba* noodles symbolize a long life. *Soba* noodles are made from buckwheat flour, and are sometimes colored with green tea or beets. The noodles can be bought dried or fresh. *Soba* is very popular in Japan and is served cold with soy sauce and vegetables or in a hot, flavorful broth. Here's a recipe for a comforting hot bowl of noodle soup. (Makes 2 servings.)

Here's What You Need

Ingredients
- 1 vegetable bouillon cube
- ½ teaspoon (2.5 ml) of sugar
- 2 cups (.5 liter) water
- 1 scallion, chopped
- 2 teaspoons (10 ml) of soy sauce
- 1 package of bundled *soba* noodles (available in Asian supermarkets or groceries)

Equipment
- medium saucepan
- measuring cup and spoons

Here's What You Do

1 Place all the ingredients, except for the noodles, in a saucepan. Heat on low.

2 When the bouillon has dissolved, place 2 bundles of noodles in the pan and stir until the noodles are soft, about 5 minutes.

3 Pour the noodle soup into two serving bowls.

The Ancestors Return to Their Tombs

On the last day of Obon, families relight their lanterns and fires to guide the spirits back to their graves. *Dango,* rice balls made of rice flour and flavored with green tea or red bean, are prepared in their honor. In the evening, scores of families who live by the water crowd together near the shores of Osaka or Kobe, cities in Japan. Each family has a wooden boat holding tiny paper lanterns. Some families place the names of their ancestors in the boat. The lanterns are lit and the boats sail away, the hundreds of flickering lights slowly disappearing into the dark sea. The spirits of the ancestors follow the boats to their home.

Hanukkah

-ISRAEL-

On the twenty-fifth day of the lunar month of Kislev (which falls in December of the Gregorian calendar), the first month of the Jewish calendar, Israeli Jews and Jewish people everywhere hold an eight-day celebration of rededication, or restoration, which is known as *Hanukkah* (pronounced HAH-neh-kah). Each year at this time, Jewish families rededicate themselves to practicing the customs and traditions of their religion. During the eight days of Hanukkah, people get together to remember important events in Jewish history. During the celebration, they light candles in a nine-branched candleholder called a *menorah*. Hanukkah is also called the Festival of Lights.

Israelis celebrate the holiday in many of the same ways that Jews around the world do. They exchange Hanukkah cards with friends and family, eat delicious foods, sing songs, play games, and give gifts and gold-covered chocolate "coins" called *gelt.* But because Israel is a Jewish state, there are some added bonuses to celebrating Hanukkah there. Schools are closed during the eight-day holiday, and there is a torchlight relay race from Modin to Jerusalem.

The Jewish Homeland

The Jewish people have been connected to Israel since ancient times, when the Hebrews occupied parts of the land. The history of Abraham, who is considered to be the founder of the Hebrews, and his descendants is recorded in the the Old Testament of the Bible. Because of the biblical connection that the land and its people hold, Jews refer to Israel as the Holy Land. Throughout early history, the Jewish people struggled to hold on to their land and live peaceful lives, but they were met with many challenges. First the Hebrews were enslaved, then their land was conquered by many outsiders, including the Babylonians, the Greeks, and the Romans. The Jews were forced to leave their homeland.

Following the arrival of the Romans into Palestine, the Jewish people dispersed, settling in areas throughout the Middle East and Europe. They built synagogues and practiced their religion wherever they went. But they always looked forward to the day when they would be able to return to their homeland.

In the 1500s some Jews returned to Palestine (which is the name Israel was then called) to escape European prejudice. The Ottoman Turks had taken over and welcomed Jews back into the country, but many Jews wanted a nation of their own. People who worked for that goal were called Zionists. (*Zion* is an ancient word that means "for Israel.") Meanwhile, Jews continued to return to Palestine, particularly from war-torn Europe. In 1948, with the help of the United Nations, the state of Israel was created in Palestine, and Jews who had survived persecution in Europe returned to their biblical homeland. But all was not peaceful. Palestinians who had been pushed off their land and people in neighboring countries have continued to war with Israel over the land.

The Meaning of Hanukkah

Over 2,000 years ago, Palestine was ruled by King Antiochus IV, a Syrian-Greek leader. The king forbade the Jews from practicing their religion, going to temple to pray, or reading the Torah, a holy book. He commanded the Jews to honor the Greek gods. Then King Antiochus IV took over the Jewish Temple of Jerusalem and turned it into a temple to the Greek god Zeus. The Jews fought back. A small army led by Judah Maccabee defeated the king and his army, and took back their Temple. When the followers of Judah Maccabee, who were called Maccabees, went to light the sacred oil lamp in the temple, they discovered that there was only enough oil to keep the lamp burning for one day. They lit the lamp, but to their surprise it continued to burn brightly for eight days. A wonderful miracle had happened. The Jews wanted future generations to know about this miracle and the events that led up to it, so they created Hanukkah to commemorate it.

Race to Jerusalem

The most exciting and meaningful event in Israel is the torch relay race that welcomes the Hanukkah season. The race begins in Modin (pronounced MOH-din), where the Maccabees lived and their war began, twelve miles outside of Jerusalem. Thousands of people come to watch. A bonfire is set and the first runners light their torches. Each racer runs with the torch, then passes it on to other waiting relay racers. People from all over the country come to see the passing of the torch as it makes its way to its final destination, the Old Wall at Jerusalem. When the final racer makes his way to Jerusalem, he is greeted by welcoming cheers from thousands of Israelis. The runner passes the torch to a rabbi who lights the *hannukkiya,* the eight-branched menorah that sits on top of the ancient wall in Old Jerusalem. After the rabbi says a prayer, Hanukkah officially begins.

The torchlight ceremony commemorates the memory of those who fought for freedom and their courage. Hanukkah torches also shine brightly in Masada, where other freedom fighters lived. All over the country, there are parades or pilgrimages to many Maccabean sites in Modin. Israelis also visit other holy places, such as the Old City of Jerusalem.

The Hanukkah Celebration

The celebration begins each day at dusk. Each night of Hanukkah, Israelis light one candle for each of the days the lamp burned in the temple of Jerusalem. They also light one more candle, the *shammash,* which is a candle used to light the others. The shammash is lit first.

On the first night of the holiday, a family member is chosen to light the shammash and the first Hanukkah candle. While the candles are being lit the family recites blessings or sings songs dedicated to the miracle that happened over 2,000 years ago. On the second night, another family member lights the second candle and relights the first. More songs are sung or prayers recited. This ritual continues until all the candles have been lighted. The menorah is often placed near a window so that the rest of the world can see it and learn about the miracle.

Nightly, at sundown, synagogues also hold candle-lighting ceremonies during the holiday. Many Israelis go to temple, then enjoy the delicious powdered jelly doughnuts that are given out, which is an Israeli tradition. You can see the spirit and the joy of the festival throughout Israel. Flickering menorahs—ceramic, bronze, silver—shine brilliantly in the windows of homes and businesses around the entire country. All of Israel flickers with lights.

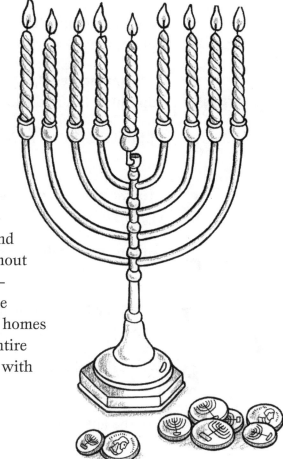

Hanukkah Foods

Each night after the candles are burned, Israelis sit down to enjoy some special foods. During this time, as always, they "keep kosher," which means that they only eat foods that are allowed under Jewish law. For example, Jews may not eat shellfish or pork, and other animals must be butchered in a certain way. Jews must also avoid eating certain foods together, such as milk and meat. According to Jewish law, meat symbolizes death and milk is a sign of life, and therefore, the two should never be mixed together.

Israelis eat a lot of fried foods during Hanukkah. The frying oil is a symbol of the sacred oil found in the Jewish temple by the Maccabees that kept the lamp burning for eight miraculous days. Bakeries are very busy weeks before Hanukkah, and people stand in long lines waiting to get a box of delicious, warm *sufganiyot* (Israeli jelly doughnuts). Another traditional dish is potato *latkes,* or pancakes. Other foods served might be an Israeli salad—chopped cucumber, tomatoes, and green onions in olive oil—cheeses, and fruits.

Potato Latkes

Most Israeli children look forward to making and eating latkes during the holiday. Have fun making these pancakes for your friends and family this Hanukkah. (Makes 6–8 latkes.)

Here's What You Need

Ingredients

- 4 medium to large potatoes
- half an onion
- 2 eggs
- 1/4 cup (59 ml) flour
- 1 teaspoon (5 ml) salt
- 1/4 teaspoon (1.25 ml) pepper
- 1 cup (237 ml) vegetable oil for frying
- applesauce
- sour cream

Equipment

- serving plate
- paper towels
- potato peeler
- grater
- mixing bowls
- sharp knife
- whisk or fork
- measuring cups and spoons
- large frying pan
- spatula
- adult helper

Here's What You Do

1 Line a serving plate with paper towels.

2 Ask your adult helper to peel and then grate the potatoes into a mixing bowl.

3 Ask your adult helper to chop the onions to make 1/4 cup (59 ml). Add the onions to the bowl.

4 Put the eggs into a large bowl and lightly beat.

5 Mix the chopped onions and grated potatoes into the egg mixture.

6 Add the flour, salt, and pepper to the batter. Stir well.

7 Have an adult heat one cup of vegetable oil in a large frying pan.

8 When the oil is hot, drop spoonfuls of the batter into the pan.

9 Fry the latkes until they're brown on each side, about three to four minutes to a side.

10 Use the spatula to move the cooked latkes on the plate lined with paper towels to drain excess oil.

11 Serve the latkes warm with a little applesauce or sour cream.

A Dreidel Game

During Hanukkah, children like to play a game with dreidel (pronounced DRAY-del). A dreidel is a spinning top with four sides. Each side has a Hebrew letter on it—*nun, gimmel, hey,* and *poh.* These letters are in the words *nes gadol hayah poh,* which means "a great miracle happened here."

The dreidel game began when King Antioch IV forbade the Jews from studying their holy book, the Torah. Many Jews had secretly memorized passages from the Torah and they would help one another study. When they heard the Syrian-Greek soldiers coming, they would pull out their spinning tops and pretend to be playing a game.

DREIDEL

The dreidel game is a lot of fun and can be played by two or more people.

Here's What You Need

- [ ] 2 4¹/₄-by-5¹/₂-inch (10.7-by-13.97-cm) pieces of thin cardboard or posterboard
- [ ] ruler
- [ ] pencil
- [ ] scissors
- [ ] tape
- [ ] glue
- [ ] poster paint in blue and white

Here's What You Do

1 Fold the two edges of one piece of the cardboard together so the shorter edges meet. Fold the cardboard in half again. You now have four boxes.

2 Fold in half again the other way to make four rectangles. Open the cardboard. You now have eight rectangles.

3 Using the ruler, find the midpoint of the short side of one rectangle and mark it with a pencil.

4 Do the same with the remaining three rectangles on that edge of the cardboard.

5 With a ruler, draw lines from point *a* and point *c* to the midpoint (*b*). Cut the lines drawn. Do the same for the remainder of the rectangles facing you.

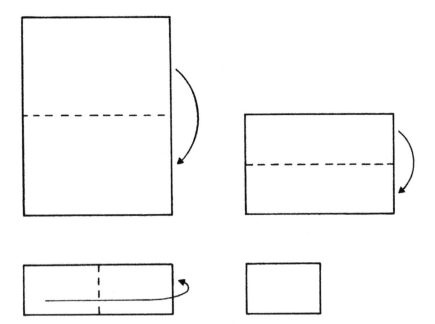

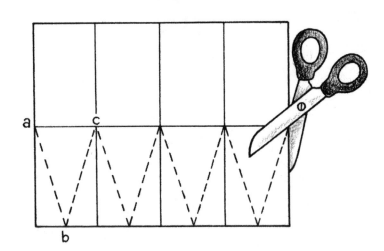

6 Fold into a box along the folded edges. The bottom will be pointed, while the top will be open. Tape the cardboard together in this shape.

7 Take the second piece of cardboard and cut a 1-inch (2.54-cm) square from each corner, leaving a cross shape.

8 Find the midpoint of the center square of the cardboard cross and mark it with a pencil.

9 Center the middle of the cross shape over the opening of your dreidel. Glue down the flaps of the cross shape onto the sides of the dreidel.

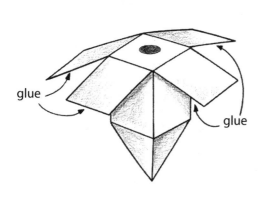

glue

glue

10 Insert a sharpened pencil through the middle of the dreidel.

11 Paint the dreidel blue and let the paint dry.

12 Draw the Hebrew characters, shown below, with white paint. Let the paint dry.

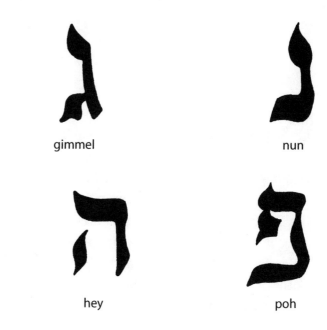

gimmel

nun

hey

poh

Here's how you play:

First each player puts one or more chocolate coins or real coins in a pile on the floor, then each player spins the top. If the dreidel lands faceup on *gimmel,* the player wins all the money; if the dreidel lands on *hey,* the player wins half the money; if a player lands on *nun,* the player does nothing; and if the player lands on *poh,* the player must add money to the pot.

Kwanzaa

-THE UNITED STATES-

Kwanzaa is an African American holiday that was created in 1966 by a civil rights leader and teacher named Dr. Maulana Karenga. The word *kwanzaa* means "first fruits" in Swahili, a language spoken in many African countries. The holiday is celebrated from December 26 to January 1. It is a joyous and festive celebration and a chance for African Americans to get together, celebrate the "fruits" cultivated by their ancestors, honor their ancestors, and think about their history, culture, and community. Some African American families celebrate other holidays, such as Christmas, at the same time that they celebrate Kwanzaa; others celebrate only Kwanzaa. Families decorate their homes for the holiday and people exchange greeting cards and gifts. Children play an important part in the celebration of Kwanzaa.

The Meaning of Kwanzaa

During the 1960s, African Americans were facing tough hurdles: they were fighting against racism, and struggling to build better communities. Dr. Karenga wanted to do something to help African Americans stay strong and come together as a community. He wanted African Americans to have a sense of pride in themselves and their people. Dr. Karenga created Kwanzaa to teach African Americans about the culture and traditions of their African ancestors. He based the rituals of Kwanzaa on ancient harvest festivals held by many different African peoples. He felt that African Americans would be inspired by the way that everyone had to work as a team in these cultures to produce the best results.

Nguzo Saba (Seven Principles)

The important messages of Kwanzaa are for African Americans to share common goals and work together to keep their communities strong. There are seven Kwanzaa principles, called *nguzo saba* (Swahili for "seven principles"), that can help African Americans achieve their goals. Each day of the weeklong festival is devoted to celebrating one of the seven principles:

Umoja (Unity): Keep the family together.

Kujichagulia (Self-Determination): Do not let others make decisions for you.

Ujima (Collective Work and Responsibility): Work together with others.

Ujaama (Cooperative Economics): Create and support black-owned businesses.

Nia (Purpose): Support the community as a whole and help other individuals in the community become the best they can be.

Kuumba (Creativity): Think of ways that will benefit the community financially and spiritually.

Imani (Faith): Believe in yourself and in others.

Preparing for the Celebration

African Americans gather important symbols to prepare for Kwanzaa. During the feast, homes are decorated with the colors red, black, and green. Red symbolizes the blood shed in blacks' long fight for freedom; black stands for the black people, and green is for the future. A flag made of those symbolic colors, called a *bendera,* is displayed along with a poster showing the seven principles of Kwanzaa.

African Americans often hang on a wall a poster of *nguzo saba,* the seven Kwanzaa principles, and the *bendera,* a flag symbolizing the struggle of their people.

The next step is to prepare the traditional Kwanzaa table. The items set on the table remind African Americans of the materials and items used by their ancestors. A *mkeka,* mat woven from straw or paper, is placed on a table. It symbolizes a strong foundation on which everything else will be added. A big cup, the *kikombe cha umoja,* is set on the mat. The cup is a symbol of togetherness. Each family member takes a drink from the water-filled cup during the celebration. Next come the *mazao,* the fruits and vegetables that symbolize the harvest or the fruits of any hard labor. *Muhindi,* corn, is a symbol for children. If there are three children in the family, three ears of corn will be placed on the *mkeka.* A very important item on the *mkeka* is a seven-branched candleholder, the *kinara,* and *mishumaa saba,* the candles that fill it. Each candle stands for one of the seven principles of Kwanzaa. A black candle is placed in the center of the holder, then three green candles are placed on the right, and three red candles on the left. The last symbol of Kwanzaa is the *zawadi,* gifts given as rewards for practicing the principles of the holiday year-round.

KWANZAA MKEKE

In Africa, a *mkeke* is a woven mat made of straw. It is a very important part of the Kwanzaa festival. It is a base for all African American traditions. For your holiday table, weave a *mkeke,* using the three colors of Kwanzaa.

Here's What You Need

- 1 11-by-17 inch (28-by-43-cm) sheet each of red, black, and green construction paper
- ruler
- scissors
- white pencil
- pencil
- glue

Here's What You Do

1 Fold the short sides of the sheet of the black construction paper in half.

2 Place your ruler against the folded edge and with your white pencil mark spaces 1 inch (2.5 cm) apart. Do the same on the opposite end of your construction paper.

3 With the pencil, draw lines connecting the marks on opposite ends of the paper.

4 Starting at the folded edge, cut along each penciled line, leaving an inch of space at the unfolded edge top of the paper.

5 Place your ruler against the long edge of the red construction paper and with your white pencil mark spaces 1 inch (2.5 cm) apart. Do the same on the opposite end of the paper.

6 With the pencil, connect the marks on the opposite edge of the paper, then cut the strips.

7 Repeat steps 5 and 6 to make strips from the green construction paper.

8 Take a red strip and weave it in and out of the cuts you made in the black construction paper.

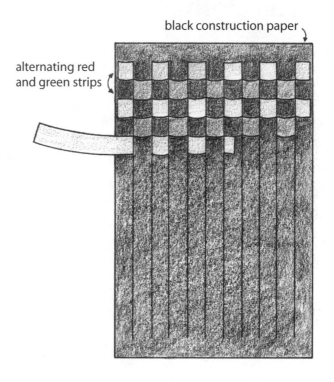

black construction paper

alternating red and green strips

9 Weave a green strip through the construction paper. Now weave a red strip. Continue weaving the papers until the mat is completed.

10 Use a little bit of glue to paste down the ends of red and green paper around the black mat.

Kwanzaa clothes

Dressing up is a fun and special part of Kwanzaa. Many African Americans wear traditional African dress. Men and boys may wear a long robe called a *kanza*, and a *kufi*, a small round hat. They may also wear a *dashiki*, a large loose-fitting colorful shirt. Women wear a *buba*, a long gown, or a *busuti*, a robe with a scarf tied at the waist. Women and girls may also wear a *gele*, a head wrap made of cloth.

kufi

kanza

dashiki

gele headwrap

busuti

buba

Habari Gani?

On the first day of Kwanzaa, children and adults gather around the table set for the celebration. Someone asks, *"Habari gani?"* What's the news? The answer is the principle for that day. *"Umoja,"* a child answers. The child lights the black candle, which symbolizes the principle Umoja, or Unity, then everyone takes a drink of water from the *kikombe,* a goblet. Afterward, the child who lit the candle talks about the meaning of Umoja. Everyone around the table talks about what Unity means to them. At the end, everyone shouts *"Harambee!"* Let's pull together!

For the next six days, a candle is lit on each day to symbolize the principle for that day. The previous day's candles are relit, too. Children discuss the meaning of each day's principle, everyone sips from the *kikombe,* and at the end of the celebration, when all seven candles have been lit, everyone shouts *"Harambee"* seven times.

On the last day of Kwanzaa, families and friends exchange *zawadi,* gifts. These gifts may be handmade, or they can be bought, but they are traditionally educational and related to African or African American history, culture, or art.

Karamu Feast

On December 31, the sixth day of Kwanzaa, families prepare a huge feast called the *karamu.* A large African cloth, such as *kente,* is placed in the middle of the floor, and dishes of food are spread out on top of it. Everyone attending the meal brings a dish. The foods served are the kinds their ancestors in Africa would have harvested: yams, corn, okra, lentils, rice, and different greens. There are also breads and biscuits, fruits and fruit drinks. Families and friends sit down to eat in the traditional African way—on pillows or cushions on the floor.

CORN BREAD

For your Kwanzaa holiday meal, try preparing a good old-fashioned corn bread. It's delicious with a meal or by itself. (Serves 4–8.)

Here's What You Need

Ingredients

- [ ] 1 cup (237 ml) yellow cornmeal
- [ ] 1 cup (237 ml) flour
- [ ] 1 tablespoon (30 ml) sugar
- [ ] 2 teaspoons (10 ml) baking powder
- [ ] a dash of salt
- [ ] 2 eggs, beaten
- [ ] ¼ cup (60 ml) vegetable oil, plus a drop for greasing the baking pan
- [ ] 1 cup milk (237ml)
- [ ] butter (optional)

Equipment

- [ ] mixing bowl and spoon
- [ ] measuring cup and spoon
- [ ] 9-by-9-by-2-inch (23-by-23-by-5 cm) square baking pan
- [ ] oven mitts
- [ ] adult helper

Here's What You Do

1 Preheat the oven to 425°F (218°C)

2 Combine the dry ingredients together in a mixing bowl. Mix well.

3 Add the eggs, vegetable oil, and milk. Mix well.

4 Grease the baking pan with a drop of vegetable oil.

5 Pour the mixture into the baking pan.

6 Ask an adult helper to put the corn bread in the oven.

7 Bake the corn bread for 20 to 25 minutes, or until golden brown on top.

8 Ask an adult to remove the corn bread from the oven and serve immediately, plain or with butter.

Index

A
Africa, 70–77, 79
African Americans, 55, 56, 114–20
Afro-Brazilians, 36, 37
ancestors, 6, 17, 79, 91, 101, 105, 114
Año Viejo (Old Year), 21–25
arts and crafts festivals, 79
Ash Wednesday, 33, 35, 54
"Auld Lang Syne," 17, 27

B
ball drop in Times Square, 28
Barbados, 78–83
bautto, 49
bead necklaces, 57
bendera, 116
Bhogi Pongal, 66
black buns, 14
black-eyed peas, 31
Boston, Massachusetts, 27
Brahma, 66
Brazil, 35–41
Bridgetown, Barbados, 82
Buddha, 100, 103
Buddhists, 99–105

C
Cajuns, 58
cakes, 14, 58–62
calendars, 4, 6, 46
calypsos, 79, 82
canals of Venice, 48, 49
candles, 106, 108–109, 116, 119
cards, greeting, 46–47
carnaval (Brazil), 35–41
carnevale (Venice), 48–53
carnival (New Orleans), 33
carnival beads, 57
chiao-tzu, 7–9
China, 5–12
Chinese calendar, 4, 6
clans, 17–18
clay pot, 80–81
cleaning ritual, 67, 101
clothes, 103, 118
coconut cooler, 40
commedia dell'arte (comedy of art), 50
corn bread, 119–120
corn dolly, 89–90
cornucopia, 89

costumes
carnevale, 49, 50
Chinese New Year, 12
Crop-Over, 82
kilts, 17
Mardi Gras, 54, 56
New Yam festival, 73
samba school flag bearers, 38
cowpeas and rice, 31–32
cows, 65, 68
Creoles, 58
Creole Wild West Tribe, 56
crests, 17–20
Crop-Over, 78–83

D
dancing, 6, 12, 73, 101, 103–104
date-nut cookies, 44–45
decorations, 89, 101, 116
dragon dance, 6, 12
dreidel game, 111–113
drums, 73–76, 79, 103
dumplings, Chinese, 7–9
Dundee cake, 14

E

Easter, 33
Ecuador, 21–25
Edinburgh, Scotland, 16, 17
Eid Mubarak greeting cards, 46–47
Eid ul-Fitr, 33, 42–47
El Día de los Reyes (Three Kings Day),
    93–98
Emperor Jade, 6
ensalada de frutas (fruit salad), 24–25

F

fasting, 33, 42
"Fat Tuesday," 33, 54
feasts, 43, 67, 83, 86, 94, 104, 119
festivals and fairs
    Año Viejo festival, 22
    Barbadian Crop-Over, 79
    Boston First Night, 27
    Ecuador, 22
    Festival of Lanterns, 101
    Festival of Lights, 106
    Festival of the Breaking of the
        Fast, 33, 42–44
    Festival of the Dead, 99–105
    Hogmanay Street Fair, 16
fiestas, 22, 93, 96
Fire Procession, 16
first-footing, 14
First Night, 27

flag bearers, 38
floats, parade, 57
football games, 31, 88
French Mardi Gras, 55
fruit salad, 24–25
fufu, 76, 77

G

games, 16, 79, 88, 111–113
garland, 69
gifts, 9, 14, 66, 94, 116, 119
ginger beer, 83
gods, 6, 63, 65, 66, 67, 70, 91
gondolas, 48, 49
Grand Canal, Venice, 48, 49
Grand Kadooment Day, 82
greeting cards, 46–47
Gregorian calendar, 4
Guayaquil, Ecuador, 22

H

"habari gani?" 119
haggis, 14
Hale, Sarah Bush, 88
Hanukkah, 106–113
Harding, Mr., 82
harvests, 63, 65, 70, 72, 78, 79, 86
Hinduism, 66
Hindus, 65–69
Hogmanay, 13–20

Hoppin' John, 31–32
hot chocolate, 95

I

Igbos, 70–77
India, 65–69
Indians (Native Americans), 56,
    58, 86
Iriji, 70–77
Islam, 43
Israel, 106–113
Italy, 48–53

J

jaggery, 66
Japan, 99–105
Jerusalem, 108
Jesus, 93, 94
Jews, 106–113
Julian calendar, 4

K

Kadooment Day, 82
karamu (feast), 119
Karenga, Maulana, 114, 115
kilars, 67
king cake, 58, 59–62
Kitchen God, 6
Koran, 43
kosher, 109
Krewe of Rex, 55

krewes, 55–56, 57
Kwanzaa, 114–20

L lai-see, 9
Lantern Festival, 6, 101
lanterns, 101–102, 105
Lent, 33, 35, 54
Lincoln, Abraham, 88
lion dance, 6, 12
Louisiana, 33, 54–62

M Macy's department store, 88
"mango of the future," 37
Mardi Gras, 33, 54–62
Mardi Gras Indians, 56
masks, 48, 49, 50–52, 55, 73
masquerades, 48, 55, 56, 73
Mattu Pongal, 68
Mecca, 43
menorah, 106, 108, 109
Mexico, 93–98
mkeke (mat), 116–18
Modin, Israel, 108
Moggallana, 103
mosques, 43
motto, 17
Mr. Harding, 82
Muhammad, 43

Muslims, 33, 42–43, 46–47
Mystic Krewe of Comus, 55

N Native Americans, 56, 58, 86, 89
New Orleans, Louisiana, 33, 54–62
New Yam Festival, 70–77
New Year's Eve, 16, 22, 24, 26–30
New Year's resolutions, 21, 27
New York City, 27, 28, 88
Nguzo Saba (Seven Principles), 115
Nigeria, 70–77
Noche Vieja (New Year's Eve), 22
noisemaker, 29–30

O Obon, 99–105
Obon-odori dances, 101, 103–104
Old Year celebration, 21–25

P Palestine, 107, 108
pantomimes, 31
paper lanterns, 101–102, 105
papier-mâché masks, 50–52
parade clubs, 55–56
parades
    Boston First Night, 27
    Chinese New Year, 6, 12
    Crop-Over, 79, 82
    Hogmanay, 16

Mardi Gras, 55–57
    Mummer's, 31
    Samba School Parade, 36
    Tournament of Roses, 31
    United States New Year, 31
    United States Thanksgiving, 88
parishes, 79
parties, 28, 48, 55, 56, 82, 96
Pasadena, California, 31
pet garland, 69
Philadelphia, Pennsylvania, 31
pie, pumpkin, 86–87
Pilgrims, 85, 86, 89
piñatas, 96–98
Pongal (celebration), 65–69
pongal (rice pudding), 65, 67–68
porta-bandeira, 38
potato latkes, 109, 110
pottery, 80–81
pumpkin pie, 86–87
puppets, 22–24

R race to Jerusalem, 107, 108
Ramadan, 33, 42
recipes
    chiao-tzu, 7–9
    corn bread, 119–120
    cowpeas and rice, 31–32

recipes (*continued*)

date-nut cookies, 44–45

ensalada de frutas (fruit salad), 24–25

ginger beer, 83

hot chocolate, 95

king cake, 59–62

pumpkin pie, 87

refresco de côco (coconut cooler), 40–41

scones, 15–16

soba noodle soup, 104

tramezzini, 52–53

refresco de côco (coconut cooler), 40–41

Rio de Janeiro, Brazil, 35–37

rosca de reyes (three kings bread), 94

S Salvador, Brazil, 36

samba, 35–38

Samba School Parade, 36

Samba schools, 36–37

Sambódromo (Sambadrome) stadium, 37

Santana dharma, 66

Saudi Arabia, 42–47

scones, 15–16

Scotland, 13–20

Scottish Highlands, 17

Seven Kwanzaa Principles, 115, 116, 119

singing, 17, 27, 79, 82, 108, 109

slaves, 36, 56, 71, 78, 79, 82

soba noodle soup, 104

spiritual celebrations, 91

spring couplets, 10–12

stick lickey game, 79

sugarcane, 78, 79, 83

sugarcane juice, 83

surnames, 18

Surya Pongal, 67

symbols, 10, 67, 89, 116

T Taiwan, 12

tartan, 17

thanksgiving celebrations, 63

Thanksgiving Day Parade, 88

three kings bread, 94

Three Kings Day, 93–98

"throwing the hammer" game, 16

throws, 57

Times Square ball drop, 27, 28

Torah, 108, 111

torchlight ceremony, 108

tramezzini, 52–53

tribes, Native American, 56

turkey dinner, 84, 86

U United States

Boston, Massachusetts, 27

Kwanzaa, 114–20

New Orleans, Louisiana, 54–62

New Year's celebration, 26–32

New York City, 27, 28

Pasadena, California, 31

Philadelphia, Pennsylvania, 31

Thanksgiving, 84–90

V Venice, Italy, 48–53

W West Africans, 58, 71

wrestling contests, 73

Y yams, 70, 71, 72, 76–77

Z Zulu Social and Pleasure Club, 55, 57